VICTORY
Choices in Reaction
by Howard Barker

Victory

Choices in Reaction

By the same author

Stage Plays

Cheek
No One Was Saved
Alpha Alpha
Edward, The Final Days
Stripwell
Claw
Fair Slaughter
The Love of a Good Man
That Good Between Us
The Hang of the Gaol
Birth on a Hard Shoulder
The Loud Boy's Life
No End of Blame
The Poor Man's Friend

T.V. Plays

Cows
Mutinies
Prowling Offensive
Conrod
Heroes of Labour
Russia
All Bleeding
Credentials of a Sympathizer
Heaven
Pity in History

Radio Plays

One Afternoon on the 63rd Level of the North Face
  of the Pyramid of Cheops the Great
Henry V in Two Parts
Herman with Millie and Mick

Playscript 104

VICTORY
Choices in Reaction

Howard Barker

JOHN CALDER · LONDON
RIVERRUN PRESS · NEW YORK

First published in Great Britain 1983 by
John Calder (Publishers) Ltd.,
18, Brewer Street,
London W1R 4AS

and in the USA 1983 by
Riverrun Press Inc.,
175 Fifth Avenue,
New York, NY 10010

Copyright © Howard Barker, 1983

All performing rights in this play are strictly reserved and
applications for performances should be made to:
Judy Daish Associates Ltd.,
122 Wigmore Street,
London W1H 9FE

No performance of this play may be given unless a licence has been obtained
prior to rehearsal.

ALL RIGHTS RESERVED

British Library Cataloguing in Publication Data
Barker, Howard
    Victory—(Playscript series; 104)
    I. Title
    822'.914   PR6052.A6485

SUBSIDISED BY THE
Arts Council
OF GREAT BRITAIN

ISBN 0 7145 3986 4 paperbound

Any paperback edition of this book whether published simultaneously
with, or subsequent to, the hardback edition is sold subject to the
condition that it shall not, by way of trade, be lent, resold, hired
out, or otherwise disposed of, without the publisher's consent, in
any form of binding or cover other than that in which it is published.

No part of this publication may be reproduced, stored in a retrieval
system, or transmitted in any form by any means, electronic,
mechanical, photocopying, recording or otherwise, except brief
extracts for the purpose of review, without the prior written
permission of the publisher and the copyright holder.

Typeset in 9/10 point Times by Gedset of Ged Lennox Design, Cheltenham.
Printed and bound by the Hillman Press, Frome, England

CONTENTS

	Page
Act One	1
Scene One	*1*
Scene Two	*3*
Scene Three	*9*
Scene Four	*17*
Scene Five	*23*
Act Two	39
Scene One	*39*
Scene Two	*46*
Scene Three	*50*
Scene Four	*54*
Scene Five	*62*

Characters

BRADSHAW	The Widow of a Polemicist
SCROPE	A Secretary
CHARLES STUART	A Monarch
NODD	His Intimate Friend
DEVONSHIRE	A Mistress
BALL	A Cavalier
MCCONOCHIE	A Surgeon
CROPPER	Daughter of Bradshaw
BOOT	A Soldier
SHADE	"
WICKER	"
GAUKROGER	A Captain
ROAST	A Civil Servant
CLEGG	The Poet Laureate
SOUTHWARK	A Male Landowner
CLEVELAND	A Female Landowner
PONTING	A Court Official
HAMPSHIRE	A Male Landowner
BRIGHTON	A Female Landowner
SOMERSET	A Male Landowner
DERBYSHIRE	" "
GLOUCESTERSHIRE	" "
FEAK	A Republican
PYLE	A Republican Woman
EDGBASTON	A Radical Preacher
HAMBRO	A Banker
MOBBERLEY	A Builder
PARRY	A Stockbroker
UNDY	An Exporter
STREET	A Lawyer
MONCRIEFF	A Minister
GWYNN	A Prostitute
FOOTMAN	To Devonshire
MILTON	A Genius
BEGGARS	

Victory was first performed, in a version for ten actors, by the Joint Stock Theatre Company, in association with the Royal Court Theatre, at the Gardner Centre, Brighton, on February 17th, 1983, with the following cast. It opened at the Royal Court on 25th March, 1983

BRADSHAW/CLEVELAND
DEVONSHIRE/CROPPER/GWYNN/PYLE
BALL/HAMPSHIRE/STREET/MONCRIEFF
NODD/SHADE/FEAK/BEGGAR
HAMBRO/GAUKROGER/FOOTMAN
DARLING/PONTING/BANK GUARD/BEGGAR
CLEGG/MOBBERLEY/ROAST
SCROPE/SOMERSET/UNDY
MCCONOCHIE/BOOT/SOUTHWARK/PARRY/BEGGAR
CHARLES/EDGBASTON/MILTON

Julie Covington
Eleanor David
Kenny Ireland
Peter Lovstrom
David Lyon

Adam Robertson
Hugh Ross
Toby Salaman

Martin Stone
Nigel Terry

Directed by Danny Boyle
Designed by Deirdre Clancy

ACT ONE

Scene One

A field. A man enters.

SCROPE. I know I swore. I know I promised. On the Bible. And because I can take or leave the Bible, got your child in and told me put my two hands on her cheeks and looking in her eyes say I would not disclose this place. No matter what the madness, what the torture, leave you underneath the nettles, safe. I did. I know I did. *(He points to a place. SOLDIERS enter with spades.)*
BOOT. A scythe, John!
SHADE. Oh, the cunning of 'im, oh, the artfulness, sneakin' 'is bits under the lush at night . . .
BOOT. Mind the thistles.
WICKER. Now tell us 'e is twelve foot deep.
SCROPE. Twelve feet at least . . .
WICKER. Twelve foot, Michael! And the sun like the bald baker's bollocks!
BOOT *(to* DARLING*).* No, a scythe, you know a scythe, do you?
WICKER. Ow! Thistle got me!
SHADE. This is nothin' to what we 'ave 'ad, is it? Draycott was under fifteen ton a rock.
BOOT. At low water.
SHADE. At low water. We was in and out like the mad vicar's dick.
BOOT *(to* DARLING*).* Thank you. That is a scythe.
SHADE. An' Rouse, who 'ad imself stuck in the street, 'alf in the pavement, 'alf in a shop —
BOOT *(scything).* Mind yer legs!
GAUKROGER. I wonder if one of you cunts would condescend to fetch my stool? In your own time, of course, at your very own cunt leisure?
BOOT. Captain's stool, John!

DARLING hurries out.

GAUKROGER. I hate to trouble you cunts, I honestly do.
SHADE. This draper says, 'What! The corpse of a rebel under my shop! Well, I never! 'ow did that come about!' So we go through 'is bedrooms, an' is trunks, an' 'is girls. And there it is. Milton. Latin dirt.
GAUKROGER *(as* DARLING *brings in a stool).* Thank you. I have commanded some cunts, but you take the cunt biscuit.
SHADE. So we slit it, this draper's long nose. For misuse of the highway. 'Well I never! Well, I never!' 'e says . . .
BOOT *(scything).* Mind yer legs.
GAUKROGER. A stool, Mr Scrope? These cunts will be at it all day. *(*SCROPE *shakes his head.)* Who had my sunshade? *(They are digging.)* My sunshade? *(The clash of shovels.)* I do love the way they pretend to be deaf. They really are such extraordinary cunts.
BOOT. Captain's sunshade! *(*DARLING *goes out.)*
GAUKROGER. We never had one out of a field. Under the whispering cow shit and adulterous hips. Gob open to clay and the milkmaid's hot little puddle. But in sight of church steeple, I notice. How picturesque he was and diligent. Was he, Mr Scrope? Cunt picturesque your master? *(*SCROPE *bursts into tears.)* The flies are such cunts here. Would one of you run for a whisk?

Scene Two

A room. A WOMAN *and two* OFFICERS *of the crown.*

BRADSHAW. I am not asking you to sit. If I ask you to sit you will think at least she has good manners, at least she does things properly, she keeps things clean. I do not wish to do things properly or keep them clean. What do you want?

ROAST. I have to inform you —

BALL. Oh, the pontificating shitbag —

ROAST. I am instructed by His Majesty's —

BALL. Oh, the pontificating shitbag —

ROAST. May I just get this —

BALL. No, she is though, isn't she, a most pontificating bag of shit, Brian —

ROAST. If I could just —

BALL. No. Laying aside the instructing and informing for a minute, you have to marvel at her poopy aspect. I do. I have to marvel at it, all her straight back and white linen, her simple dignity and so on, it makes me want to kick the table through the window —

ROAST. I cannot see the point of making this —

BALL. I haven't finished yet! *(He goes to her.)* Brian is for being nice. Brian is ice cold and happy. But Brian never swagged his hours with the bints of Calais. I will be rude because I have lost fifteen years! Oh, my breath smells, my breath smells and she winces! Yours does not, does it, breathe on me, breathe on me —

ROAST. Andrew —

BALL. Oh, breathe on me your English breath, sweeter than roses, but then you have had English gardens to wipe your rump against, I have not but I am not angry, no, I'm not, I have licked Frenchmen's bums for nourishment and Spaniards' crotches! Breathe on me, breathe on me, do, when you stand there icy in your purity I could really dagger you with my old cavalier dick, that or murder, carry on informing, Billy. *(He walks away.)* Carry on!

ROAST. Mrs Bradshaw, the Government is in possession of your husband's body.

BALL. Oh, Brian is so poop official! We have the rat-gnawed, stinking thing

you clutched in bed once. That is what we have. What stuck up you when the cold mood took him, when God commanded fuck thy spouse or what you Bible-suckers term it, him who made you buck or whimper, is a nest of worms now and in our possession. Did you see the bollocks, Brian? I did, I thought them very mean and shrivelled little blobs, no parasite would touch them **I wish I could be more offensive I really do.** *(She is rigid.)* Oh, don't stand there like a mask of honour, I shall slap you. Did you swallow him or is that against the scriptures? I shall slap her if she looks like that!
BRADSHAW.   How would you have me look?
BALL.   Not like that!
ROAST.   His body is to be hung in London. His head spiked and exhibited.
BRADSHAW.   Why?
ROAST.   It was in the King's conditions. He would not return without his father's murderers be on display.
BALL.   There is a hole in your stocking, you slag.
BRADSHAW.   How long before I can collect and bury him?
ROAST.   There is no possibility of burial.
BRADSHAW.   What?
ROAST.   The pieces must be left to freely disintegrate.
BRADSHAW.   What!
BALL.   There is a hole in your stocking, I said.
BRADSHAW.   That is so disgusting! What?
BALL.   No, it is the hole that is disgusting, with its sixpence of white flesh —
ROAST.   **I think we ought to cut this out.** *(He stares at* BALL. BALL *shrugs.)*
BALL.   All right.
BRADSHAW.   Let me bury him. When the public's done with him.
ROAST.   I can't.
BRADSHAW.   Come on, when they have spat their mouths dry, surely?
ROAST.   The orders are the pieces be —
BRADSHAW.   Yes, but when they drop, the limbs, they can —
ROAST.   I only repeat —
BRADSHAW.   I know, but then, when they are in the gutter, then I —
ROAST.   You would need to petition —
BRADSHAW,   Oh, come on, can I pick his bits or not! *(Pause.)* They knew this. Which is why they laid in such strange places. On the seashore and so on. Knew their bits would be hunted . . .
ROAST.   This is a new world, Mrs. I was at Worcester for the Parliament. But in the end it had to stop.
BRADSHAW.   Why?

ROAST. Why, because —
BRADSHAW. Yes, why!
ROAST. Because what was needed had been done. And all the rest was chaos.
BRADSHAW. I disagree.
ROAST. You disagree, but people cannot swallow all the change you and your husband wanted —
BRADSHAW. I disagree.
ROAST *(going to leave).* Thank you for your hospitality.
BRADSHAW. What hospitality! There was none!
BALL. One night, I shan't say when, someone, I shan't say who, may toss a flaming haybale through your glass, and up will go your smart, dark privilege, the spotless boards and so discreet few flowers in the oh-so-very-unostentatious bowl . . . there has been burning up and down the country, singeing rebels' widows in their empty beds, the odour of the stale old crutch and knicker . . .
BRADSHAW. There is a sort of cleanliness in you. A sort of honour in your vileness I can understand. But you —

She looks to ROAST.

BALL. Ugh, she flatters me! Ugh! Off! Flattery! *(He pretends to wipe himself.* ROAST *goes out.)* I will fuck you, shall I? Say and I will. *(She looks away.)* They say you killed old love in England. You never! *(He goes to the door.)* I shall come back. And give you a poem. *(He leaves. A young man enters, warily.)*
MCCONOCHIE. I would have come down, but what help would I have been? It might have made them worse. I don't like foul language. Nor do you, of course. Are you crying? So I listened with the door half open, and my book on my knees. It was about blood. I would have come down in the event of violence. Blood has coloured pieces in it. It is actually not red beneath a microscope. **I don't see how I can be educated if there is no peace and quiet!**
BRADSHAW. I'm sorry.
MCCONOCHIE. I have wished — if only you knew how I wished — my father had been a grocer. You cannot know how I envy the children of grocers.
BRADSHAW. Yes.
MCCONNOCHIE. There is no prospect of progress in science or art without complete and utter stability. The universities are utterly disorganized! I may not get a place!
BRADSHAW. I know.

MCCONOCHIE.   I am not a political person and it is most unjust! *(Pause.)* Did they frighten you? I would have come down but I hate bad language and anyway you are so very strong. I do admire you. The things you can take and cry hardly ever. When I am blown haywire by interruptions. You are so resilient.
BRADSHAW.   They are sticking his head on a spike.
MCCONOCHIE.   Does that hurt you?
BRADSHAW.   No, no, it's only a head, it's only my husband's rotten old head, I often wanted to put it on a spike myself, what does it matter if your father is hung on a gate?
MCCONOCHIE.   You are getting emotional, aren't you? I can tell.
BRADSHAW.   What's a gate? What's a spike?
MCCONOCHIE.   You are.
BRADSHAW.   **It's his head.**
MCCONOCHIE.   Yes. Yes. But when you love someone — I don't know this — I have not actually loved — but when you love — it is not the flesh, is it, that one loves? Am I being indelicate?
BRADSHAW.   **I loved his head.**
MCCONOCHIE.   Yes, but I think one needs to examine what we mean by —
BRADSHAW.   **I do not** —
MCCONOCHIE.   All right, you do not, but —
BRADSHAW.   **Your dad's head.** *(Pause.)*
MCCONOCHIE.   Please, you mustn't be angry with me.
BRADSHAW.   No.
MCCONOCHIE.   Or shout. I do not see the point of shouting. Things are difficult enough without recourse to shouting.
BRADSHAW.   Yes, I'm sorry.
MCCONOCHIE.   I could shout as well. There are plenty of things I would like to shout about. I could lie down on the floor and cry. But I don't, do I?
BRADSHAW.   No. You don't.
MCCONOCHIE.   I have my problems too. I want to be a doctor. How am I going to be a doctor? You must help me, please. I am only eighteen. I do think you might give me some advice. *(Pause.)*
BRADSHAW.   We knew this would happen one day. We knew, while we argued in his little room, the ground was going from under our feet, on late summer evenings crossing the lawn, felt the threat in the shadows under the trees, and the mockery of the placid fountain. So he made me swear to bury him in an unmarked spot, in a field where he'd sat, very deep where nothing would come to abuse him. And you, I created like this, to spare you pain. What more can a mother do for her child? No ardour to be bruised, no

passion to be beaten for. A cold armouring of the eyes, the slowest of heart beats, and a tongue whose habit is to lie low in the mouth, dark as a bottom-fish, not red or roaring and at the end, ripped out. I think you will survive, my dear little blue-eyed boy . . . *(He turns away. Pause.)*
MCCONOCHIE. I am thinking of changing my name.
BRADSHAW. Good.
MCCONOCHIE. And leaving. *(Pause.)* I am sorry to bring this up now —
BRADSHAW. No, bring it up now —
MCCONOCHIE. I think it would be hypocritical if I spared your feelings today only to wound them tomorrow. I do think that would by hypocritical, don't you?
BRADSHAW. I hate tact and wariness . . .
MCCONOCHIE. I do, too.
BRADSHAW. Idiot kindliness.
MCCONOCHIE. Yes, yes!
BRADSHAW. Off with that now. Ditch pity! Ditch fuss.
MCCONOCHIE. I do like you. *(Pause.)* I am going to Scotland and calling myself McConochie.
BRADSHAW. A very good name. Ideal for a surgeon.
MCCONOCHIE. That's what I thought.
BRADSHAW. I am very proud of you. I mean that. Now pack your bag and go.
MCCONOCHIE. Now?
BRADSHAW. Yes now. I have done my best by you. Please go.
MCCONOCHIE. What — just —
BRADSHAW. Go. *(Pause. Then he turns and leaves. He passes* CROPPER, *who enters.)* They have found him. And stuck his head on a pole. *(*CROPPER *goes to her, embraces her.)* Through his brain. His poor brain. An old spike. *(She parts from her.)* Or not, do you think? I say brain, but that's silly, that really is silly, the brain I'd have thought, being soft —
CROPPER. Shh —
BRADSHAW. The very first thing to rot, I expect, I imagine would —
CROPPER. Don't imagine —
BRADSHAW. I want to imagine! Would go liquid or possibly — I have not seen a brain — dry up like a nut — a rattling nut —
CROPPER. Shh!
BRADSHAW. . . . in the skull — a pebble — or imagine —
CROPPER. Don't imagine —
BRADSHAW. I will imagine! Stop telling me not to imagine! Alternatively, a skull full of muck, which if tipped, or tilted, would drip through the eyes,

would weep its own brains out, cry muck down your skirt, splash dirty intellect on stockings and shoes —
CROPPER.   We want you to move in with us.
BRADSHAW.   His scrotum, though shrivelled, evidently was intact —
CROPPER.   The spare room —
BRADSHAW.   . . .his scrotum —
CROPPER.   Please —
BRADSHAW.   . . .after how many years? Did you see it? I saw it occasionally, though not in the light, his ardour was strictly nocturnal and grew rare with the strain, they will see it more clearly than I did, see it in hot sun and white light, his thing on some gate, his thing there for pelting and pecking, no, I shan't move in with you, your piety really makes me a bit sick. But thank you. Thank you, and thank you again.
CROPPER.   Mother —
BRADSHAW.   Oh, didn't I say thank you enough? My manners are in disarray —
CROPPER.   I only want to help.
BRADSHAW.   Yes . . . *(Pause.)* He would have had you study Latin. Was all for giving you a tutor. I stopped that. Leave her dark, I said, bovine, religious and clean. Then she will survive, and fuck with a farmer. I cannot tell you how glad I am so many of my children died. I should have had to do this six times. Six times indeed!
CROPPER.   That is very hurtful. But I shall always love you.
BRADSHAW.   Yes, you would do. The more hurtful I am the more you love me. It is all part of being bovine, religious and clean.
CROPPER.   I am not bovine!
BRADSHAW.   You are bovine. You are breasts and milk and belly, moist and passionate as stables and wet fields. No Latin, but red, oh red inside!
CROPPER.   I think you have gone mad.
BRADSHAW.   Yes. Now blot me out with pigs and children. And when the boots come up the pathway, give them your own bread and beer and jam, and they will see in your eyes your harmlessness. They will!
CROPPER *(bitterly).*   I will visit you tomorrow.
BRADSHAW.   **He had such a horror of being dug!** *(*CROPPER *turns away, in tears, goes out.)* Oh, sob, run away and sob! The one will never cry and the other never stops! **I should not have been given children!** *(Pause.)* I will bring you back. I will get your bits, your chops and scrag, your offal and your lean cuts, I will collect them. I will bring your poor bald head away that hurt me so much with its arguments.

Scene Three

The KING OF ENGLAND *enters a room.*

CLEGG. Oh, see the shadows flee the land!
The dark hour gone, and the dread hand,
The envy of the world our situation,
Ecstasy and coronation!
SOUTHWARK. I'm pissed on pomp, look at me, I'm pig hot in this ponce stuff! It's all right for you, your knockers hang out in the breezes . . .
CLEGG. Our star, our moon, our radiant sun
Like orbs of wisdom, lo, he comes!
And through our joyous, ringing city
Rides his chariot of divinity!
CLEVELAND. I never saw more dug, more boob out, like a market of fresh tit, I thought, the Abbey was a tit market, pew after pew, I never felt more like a nibble at the fruit, blew my eyes hither and thither, screwed in squint I was . . .
HAMBRO. His father hovered, saw him hovering, I thought, behind the altar, Charles the martyr, noble Stuart . . .
CLEGG. With fountain and with firework write his name,
In flower scented of his honour do the same,
Bird chants, the infant gurgles and bee hums
Oh, Charles in all his glory comes!
CHARLES. I did not actually like my dad. My dad who kept his cock dry for my mother, my mother who was a bint in essence but would shag monsignors only with her eyes, all the silliness of confession-boxes and monsignors' knobs. I adore my mother, I revere my mother, but she was an unfulfilled bint actually. And my father was in any case a sod. So there. You cannot wonder at the revolution. I never wondered at it. I think any nation governed by a bint and a sod will rise in protest, I said so at the time.
CLEGG. Rejoice, rejoice, this is our day,
Leave labour, toil, depart the fray,
Both God and Reason annointeth us
Corolingus noble, Corolingus just!
CHARLES. But my father would complicate matters by being a saint as well as a sod. A most peculiar combination. Peculiar and incomprehensible. I am

neither peculiar nor incomprehensible. I am a male bint pure and simple. I assure you, there is no better stimulus to loyalty than for an apprentice to be molly shagging only minutes after I have left her off. He grasps your flesh, he shares your monarchy. *(He turns to* HAMBRO.*)* Is that the head?
HAMBRO. *(looking out the window).* It's Bradshaw, yes.
CHARLES. There is shagall left of it.
PONTING. He is three years dead and the field was wet.
CHARLES. I will chuck skittles at it. Lower the window. I will head shy.
PONTING *(calling).* SKITTLES!
CLEVELAND. Oh, what's Charlie up to, and with the annointment still damp on his forehead! Shall we come?
CLEGG. Now grows my voice thin —
HAMPSHIRE. Good, I have a skinful of yer poetry —
CLEGG. . . .imagination sheer amaze,
My lyre expires from excess of praise,
The hours tarry, drag their feet for fun,
Delay your journey they plead of the sun!
SOMERSET. Shall we come there?
CHARLES. I head shy! I head shy!
CLEVELAND. Oh, look, a bonze all rotten underneath the window . . .
BRIGHTON. Where?

They crowd at the window.

CLEVELAND. You are leaning on me.
BRIGHTON. Ugh!

They peer in silence.

CHARLES. Is it true he wore an iron hat at my father's trial, for fear of murder?
DERBYSHIRE. And a chain vest, certainly.
GLOUCESTERSHIRE. I think you have in that one picture all the vanity and squirming terror of a man who dares to kill his master. Probably a puddle of his poop lay on the usurper's bench at the adjournment.
HAMBRO. Yet we should not resent him.
CHARLES. How's that, Hambro? How not resent him?
HAMBRO. To kill the king is no bad thing provided there follows restoration. It honours monarchy. Is proof of indispensibility.
CHARLES *(coldly).* Where is my duchess? I must grasp her arse.
NODD. Oh, Pam, dear, hither and bring your bum!
PONTING. Lady Devonshire!

NODD. Charlie, what is Hambro?
CHARLES. Billy? Billy is the banker.
NODD. I'd not go chase the clap with him, would you, love?
CHARLES. Not on your belly.
PONTING. The skittles come! The skittles!
CLEGG. The evening falls, by obligation,
Spoils the humour of our situation —
HAMPSHIRE. Oh, fuck this chanting!
CLEGG. Come night or storm we shall not move
Out of the sunlight of our monarch's love!
DEVONSHIRE. I'm here.
CHARLES. Oh, Nodd, am I not a poor male bint, wiping my knob on swan and cockatoo, draping the silk over my rump?
NODD. Now, now, this is the time of your life, silly!
CHARLES. Bradshaw cropped his hair and wore no wig, and when he pissed did not wince, I dare say, no tart came near his thing —
PONTING *(offering a tray).* Skittles?
CHARLES. ...did it — *(He takes one.)* near — your - thing? *(He chucks one.)*
DEVONSHIRE. I'm here.
CHARLES. You may all chuck now, and my hag, let her fling at the regicide's bonze!

They begin throwing in earnest.

DEVONSHIRE *(to* SOUTHWARK*).* What are we doing?
SOUTHWARK. Pelting.
CHARLES. The trunk's on Blackfriars, the legs on the Strand. Come on, chuck!
NODD. Oh, I 'it 'im!
GLOUCESTERSHIRE. He spun! I touched him, he spun!
CLEVELAND. The eyeballs! The eyeballs are watching us, ugh!
HAMPSHIRE. Knock him round, then, knock him round!
DEVONSHIRE. What are we doing, exactly?
NODD. Jaw dropped! Did yer see it?
DEVONSHIRE. I think I'll lie down.
CHARLES. Oh, no, my duchess, my duchess will chuck like a man —
DEVONSHIRE. Oh, must I?
CHARLES *(propelling her forward to the window).* Must I, must I, she says...
PONTING. **More skittles!**

The SERVANT *runs out.*
DERBYSHIRE. Oh, Teddy —
NODD. Oh, bad chucking, Ted —
HAMPSHIRE. My arm is rheumatic —
DERBYSHIRE. His arm is rheumatic —
NODD. Terrible chucking —
CLEGG. Genius lay down thy arrogance here,
 Martial ardour undo thy mask of fear,
 Virgins, youths, pale from celebration
 Mock thy stern countenance across the nation!
DEVONSHIRE. Charlie, you are hurting my arse . . .
CHARLES. Get me then, get me in your hand —
HAMPSHIRE. I struck! I did, see! Shook on its spike!
DEVONSHIRE. Look, do you want me to throw or not?
GLOUCESTERSHIRE. Clipped him! Clipped him on the ear!
BRIGHTON. Oh, the ear drops off!
DEVONSHIRE. Because I cannot if —
CHARLES. Oh, tight in your hand!
DEVONSHIRE. I am —
CHARLES. Tighter!
NODD. Oh, poor little ear! 'is little ear, look!
CHARLES. Tighter yet!
DEVONSHIRE. Ouch!
GLOUCESTERSHIRE. Cracked him! He's down!
NODD. 's down!
CLEGG. Come nymphs, come satyrs to our court,
 Old Thames thy hoary locks disport,
 And Time delay thy pouring glass,
 This gilded hour wastes too fast!
CLEVELAND. Horrible dust stuff flew away . . .
BRIGHTON. Dust stuff, Harry —
PONTING *(hanging out the window).* It's down in the yard . . .
HAMPSHIRE. Down, Charlie . . .
NODD. Bob done it.
CHARLES. I done too, quicker than I wanted . . .
PONTING *(peering).* Still in one bit, I'll be buggered . . . !
CHARLES. Out now, all of you . . .
CLEGG. Monarchy, our ancient treasure,
 Restores our joy in lavish measure —
BRIGHTON. Did you see that, Harry, grey stuff fly out the head?

SOUTHWARK. I been listening to Sam's bum-ache, ain't I?
CLEGG. And spreading dazzling luminosity,
Irradiates our curiosity!
CHARLES. Out now! Did you hear me?
NODD. Out?
CHARLES. Yes, even you, Nodd —
CLEVELAND. Out?
CHARLES. Yes, you know the word, madam, meaning the contrary of in —
PONTING. We are due on the river in fifteen —
CHARLES. Oh, listen, who is the monarch here? Who wears the ermine bum-fluff, me! I have been down, ain't I, in sight of the tit of England, got the oil of Christ on me, out then when I say it, Out! *(They depart.)* Not you!

He grabs DEVONSHIRE'S *wrist. They are alone.*

DEVONSHIRE. Charlie, I must wash my hand —
CHARLES. No.
DEVONSHIRE. I am sticky —
CHARLES. Lick it, then, cats do — *(She turns away.)* **I am a clown!**
DEVONSHIRE. Oh, dear . . .
CHARLES. **A clown, madam!** *(He walks up and down.)* Why do I? My little sprig, my little green shoot, poor little flower of my dignity, piss on it, why? It will whither, won't it? Go a monkey to my grave!
DEVONSHIRE. I hope you aren't going to be deep . . .
CHARLES. This prancing wig and whatnot, garters and the royal etcetera, why!
DEVONSHIRE. Do up your fly.
CHARLES. No, let it out!
DEVONSHIRE. Oh, God he is going to tear his raiment . . .
CHARLES. Garments down! Out bum! Out all the old flesh, grey and bedroom stale the human meat! *(He flings off his wig and trousers.)*
DEVONSHIRE. I am not looking. *(She turns resolutely away.)*
CHARLES. Hear me, please!
DEVONSHIRE. You are always like this when you've come.
CHARLES. Yes, it is the only time I see things.
DEVONSHIRE. It is a great burden to everyone else. This is your coronation.
CHARLES. A burden! A burden, she says! Truth is such a nuisance, better tuck it down somewhere, put some swan down on it, stuff it under cockatoo, a sash, a ribbon on it, quick! Madam, I have frigged my way through Europe, banging in the gardens, banging in the maze, how long can I — this — I am forty-seven — this — this — I am a red-bummed monkey!
DEVONSHIRE. Blue-bummed.

CHARLES. Blue-bummed, is it?
DEVONSHIRE. Their bums are blue.
CHARLES. Exotic-bummed in any case, to catch the glance of weary English eyes, and antic, very antic up my bars. **For whom!**
DEVONSHIRE. I am going to wash my hands.
CHARLES. I do not wonder the Emperor of Madagascar sent me baboons. I though him at the time just black and savage sending me baboons to augment my coronation. But now I see it, now I see his wisdom in their coloured arses! He mocks me! I meant to send a fleet to bomb his palace but parliament would not have voted it, what kind of monarchy is this? Where did they go? Some zoological place, I hope to God no one dissected them, I would see them, where are my baboons? **Rob!** *(He calls off for NODD.)* I shall wear baboon skin, on the river, by the light of firework, the royal barge shall be babooned! **Rob!** And bum paint, blue-arsed I shall be!
DEVONSHIRE. I must say I prefer you with your fist up me to this, the foul thing on your lips, altogether prefer it, do you see? Dragged out of dinners and humped in the passage before the eyes of servants, much prefer it —
NODD *(entering).* Charlie, you got yer trousers —
CHARLES. Where are my baboons?
NODD *(bewildered).* Baboons?
CHARLES. My blue-bums, from the great and absolute of Madagascar, him who rules by word and not by paper, the wit of Africa, almight black arse, find them, quick!
NODD. The barge is waitin' Charlie —
CHARLES. **Find them, tavern yob!** *(*NODD *goes out.)*
DEVONSHIRE. Your knob I understand, your knob I will bow down to, but not sentiment, not this yellow thing from underneath your tongue you dribble —
CHARLES. **Rob! And bum paint! I will droop my glistening arse for London out the prow!**
DEVONSHIRE. Oh, Charlie, come here, catch me underneath now, quick, not in my fingers, do look, look now, see I have no knicker, look . . .

Long pause, as she poses with her skirts flung up.

CHARLES. *(all passion spent).* Please tuck your cunt away. When you are not after them, they do look hideous . . .
NODD *(entering as she recovers herself).* Did you say bum-paint? *(Pause.)* What's that, exactly? *(Pause.)*
CHARLES. Pull up my trousers, Rob . . . *(*NODD *kneels.)*
DEVONSHIRE. I think you are the most insulting man.

CHARLES. Yes.
DEVONSHIRE. And loathsome.
CHARLES. Yes.
DEVONSHIRE. To the spunk, to the fart in you.
CHARLES *(to* NODD*).* The wig is over there, somewhere ...
DEVONSHIRE. To your little, weak come.
CHARLES. Yes. Now I think it's time you visited one of your estates.
DEVONSHIRE *(horrified).* Go out of London?
CHARLES. How else? Do you have estates in London? Get to your tin-mines.
DEVONSHIRE. No, Charlie ...
CHARLES Get down to Essex, then, and count your lobster-pots ...
DEVONSHIRE. Charlie, no thank you.
CHARLES. Oh, do. Do, yes. *(Pause, then she tears out.* NODD *adjusts his wig.)* Thank you, Rob. Now go down to the yard and fetch me Mr Bradshaw's head.
NODD. Do wha' —
CHARLES. Oh, now, don't quarrel! And see it washed, and the sparse hairs parted, as he would have wished, no mockery. *(*NODD *shrugs, starts to go.)*
Rob. *(he stops.)* We shall go drinking, soon. In dirty jerkins over Brixton.
NODD. Yup.

He goes out. HAMBRO *enters.*

CHARLES. And Rob! *(He reappears.)* I think, ask Lady Devonshire postpone her coach. I do not now, but a time will come I'll want her. I guarantee no sooner will she pass the toll than my knob will be up and barking for her. *(*NODD *goes out.* CHARLES *walks a little, adjusts his sash.)* What, Billy?
HAMBRO. It's time.
CHARLES. Oh, it is, is it?
HAMBRO. Time, yes, and such a shame to spoil the day. The people line the river.
CHARLES. Oh, let 'em wait. I'm king, ain't I?
HAMBRO. Indeed, but —
CHARLES. No, no, I'm the bloody monarch —
HAMBRO. Quite, but —
CHARLES. **Monarch, Monarch!** *(*HAMBRO *is silent, looks at the floor.* CHARLES *beckons him with a finger.)* Billy, what if I am barmy? I think the dad had it, you see, suppose I'm barmy?
HAMBRO. What if you're —
CHARLES. Sister-fucking — up nieces — down nephews — bad blood and

funny bones — Stuart eggs all broken in the saucepan — what then, Billy? Would yer have me quietly butchered?
HAMBRO. I prefer not to imagine —
CHARLES. Billy won't imagine! Billy won't! *(He goes close to him.)* Or don't it really matter any more? *(Pause.)* Billy, I do not like you awfully. You have such cold grey eyes and never fuck nobody. I wish I was cleverer, I would follow your tricks like the dog to the bitch's arse. I think you entertain some sort of treason.
HAMBRO. Treason?
CHARLES *(mocking)*. What! Treason! What! *(He smiles.)* No, Billy, darling, I mean I don't think you love me, do you, my flesh, the bone and blood of Charlie? Do you? Really love me?
HAMBRO. I was prime-mover in your —
CHARLES. Prime mover, oh, prime mover, yes, you would be, I never saw a man more purely prime moving, a prince among prime movers, primest of the prime you are, it clings like shit to the instep the prime mobility of you, Billy, did you not get this day for me, you did and thank you, you primed me very well, I am well primed though not exactly moved, but never mind, you primed the day, oh, thank you, Billy, but — *(He looks closely at him.)* I wish you fucked more . . . *(Pause.)* Off now. I come.

Blackout.

Scene Four

BRADSHAW'S *house at dusk.* SCROPE *enters.*

SCROPE. I sinned.
BRADSHAW. I was afraid you would appear.
SCROPE *(flinging himself down).* I sinned! I sinned!
BRADSHAW. Just at the moment I wanted to be alone, at the very moment I most needed to collect my thoughts, I knew you would appear —
SCROPE. I sinned!
BRADSHAW. And be very abject.
SCROPE. One blow!
BRADSHAW. Will you not shout, please?
SCROPE. One blow and I gave away the place! One blow and I led them to his grave!
BRADSHAW. How many blows did you want? *(Pause.)*
SCROPE. It wasn't a blow . . .
BRADSHAW. What was it, then?
SCROPE. A flick.
BRADSHAW. A flick?
SCROPE. A flick of a glove . . .
BRADSHAW. What sort of glove? A mailed glove?
SCROPE. **A Calf glove.**
BRADSHAW. Well, flicks can be painful.
SCROPE. You mock me! You mock my cowardice!
BRADSHAW. Mr Scrope, I have pain, too —
SCROPE. **My cowardice!**
BRADSHAW. What of my pain, Mr Scrope! *(He looks at her, sobs.)*
SCROPE. I have no courage . . . I have no dignity . . .
BRADSHAW. No, but you have your teeth. After the glove comes the fist, and after the fist comes the boot, and after the boot —
SCROPE. What I would not give for courage!
BRADSHAW. No. Let us chuck courage and hang on to our teeth.
SCROPE. I betrayed him!
BRADSHAW. Mr Scrope, I am beginning to think you overdo the abject rather —

SCROPE. **I betrayed him!**
BRADSHAW. You did not, then! He betrayed himself. *(Pause)*.
SCROPE. How?
BRADSHAW. By sharing his secret with a man who, in the last resort, preferred to keep his teeth.
SCROPE. There! You mock me!
BRADSHAW. Not at all. He was an appalling judge of character.
SCROPE. Well, you accuse me, then!
BRADSHAW. I accuse no one! I am done with accusing! I am done with shame, and conscience, duty, guilt, and power, all of it! All of your words, chuck out! *(Pause.)* Now, shake hands with me, I'm leaving.
SCROPE *(amazed out of crying)*. Leaving?
BRADSHAW. Yes. Now. In the dead of night. In what I stand up in. *(Pause.)* Scrope, your lip is quivvering. Do stop, you look an old man suddenly . . . *(She turns away.)*
SCROPE. Where? Where to?
BRADSHAW. London, to collect his pieces. And nowhere after that.
SCROPE. Why?
BRADSHAW. Why? Because we must crawl now, go down on all fours, be a dog or rabbit, no more standing up now, standing is over, standing up's for men with sin and dignity. No, got to be a dog now, and keep our teeth. I am crawling and barking, stalking, fawning, stealing breakfast, running when I see a stick, taken when I'm taken, pupping under hedges, being a proper four-legged bitch. *(Pause. He stares at her.)* Well, of course I shall have to learn it! Can't be a dog overnight!
SCROPE *(as she turns to go)*. I think my master's wife is ill . . .
BRADSHAW. Ill, me? I am weller than I ever was!
SCROPE. How can I see you, who was wife to the President of the Council, and walked with him in honour and in —
BRADSHAW. Oh, down I go! See! *(She goes down on all fours.)* Bow! Ow! Ow!
SCROPE. Oh, you shame him!
BRADSHAW. I shame him? What about him shaming me? Getting his ugly reason out, his great moral purpose, showing it in public, and his wisdom! Could not walk with him five minutes but he had his wisdom out, forever exhibiting his mind, was ever a mind hung out so much in public, dirty thing it was, great monster of a mind so flashed and brazenly dangled? Ugh! No, I was shamed if anybody was!
SCROPE. I think you should see a doctor.
BRADSHAW. A doctor? Don't you mean a vet?

SCROPE. You have gone mad with grief!
BRADSHAW. No, sane with it. Now, stand away from the window, I am leaving by it. There is a spy watches the door —
SCROPE. I refuse —
BRADSHAW. Now, be a good secretary and —
SCROPE. I must refuse —
BRADSHAW. Don't be silly, Scrope —
SCROPE. **I will be honourable in this at least.**
BRADSHAW. Scrope, I will push you over . . .

Pause. Then he stands aside, bitterly. She goes to climb through the window.

SCROPE. I must come, then, mustn't I? *(She looks at him.)* It is my duty.
BRADSHAW, I really do not want —
SCROPE. **I must.** *(Pause.)*
BRADSHAW. Then throw away your satchel. You won't need pen and paper on four legs.
SCROPE *(Taking out a book.)* Mr Bradshaw's 'Harmonia' I will not part with. Read it every night beneath the hedge.
BRADSHAW. Idiot.
SCROPE. Bring comfort to us in our —
BRADSHAW. Chew it, suck the moisture out the ink —
SCROPE.*(stuffing the book in a pocket).* It's gaol to have in your possession —
BRADSHAW. Quick! Someone's coming! Quick!

They climb out of the window. MCCONOCHIE *comes in holding a book.*

MCCONOCHIE *(rehearsing).* Guid morning to ye . . . is it noo a fine sky o'er the Firth of Forth . . . *(He stops.)* The capital of Scotland is Edinburgh. The Highlands are high. The Lowlands are low . . . *(He walks a little, stops.)* The sheep are in the heather . . . the coos are in the burn . . . *(He goes as if to shake hands.)* I am McConochie, surgeon of Leith . . . *(and again)* McConochie at your service, Bachelor of Medicine, Physician of Dundee . . . *(He ruminates.)* Dun-dee . . . Dun-dee . . . no, Leith. *(He procedes to a rocking chair, sits and reads.* BALL *appears at the window, climbs in.)*
BALL. Across the lawn I come, left off my boots, and sockless like a cavalier. But you will dry my poor wet feet in your lap, in your hot place, oh, excuse the cavalier in me, I know it offends but I have thought a lot of you in your cold puritan shift and come to master you like taking England back. I looked at England through a telescope from Calais thinking of your starched underthings and uncoloured face,and the smell of you, a little musty, I expect, the

musty hair of a sad-eyed puritan, oh, I shall have you shuddering with love, do reply, but very sweetly, and with dignity, no cock and cunt talk, you are not a cavalier tart, are you? Oh, the modesty of a real woman it does wonders to me, I am hard as rock . . .
MCCONOCHIE *(in terror).* I think you have come to the wrong house, sir . . .
BALL. What.
MCCONOCHIE. I think you have, sir —
BALL. **What!**
MCCONOCHIE *(jumping up).* Don't hit me, please, I am only a surgeon!
BALL *(drawing a dagger).* Oh, I stab you, I kill the rebel filth!
MCCONOCHIE *(on the ground).* Mercy!
BALL. What do you do in this stinking house? In this disgusting cleanliness? I burn it! I burn it! What do you do?
MCCONOCHIE. Surgeon, sir!
BALL *(releasing him).* I shall burn it, I shall! All this polish and this timber, I was a pig in Calais while they lorded it. Lorded it, I say lorded it, whatever they do in their stiff-gobbed manner! Who do you examine? In her starchy knicker with your prod? Where is the woman? Where is the widow of the king's assassin, the murdered saint's accuser, where's his pale wife? I did not prattle all my knob talk for your dirty doctor's ear.
MCCONOCHIE. Ow!
BALL. Where is she?
MCCONOCHIE. Don't know sir!
BALL. Get her, then, and quick about it, in her shift or naked off her pot, for all I care! *(*MCCONOCHIE *hurtles out the room.)* Oh, after I shall write a sonnet, after the fire has gone, a melancholy piece on how her sad face was like a pearl, and her hair like silvered weed flowing o'er the pillow . . .
*(*MCCONOCHIE *enters with a sheet of paper.)*
MCCONOCHIE. She's gone . . .
BALL. Gone! Oh, shit and piss! Then I have lost the cunt I wanted! *(He snatches the paper from* MCCONOCHIE. *Reads)* 'Have gone to be an animal, — what is this — 'in time of animals' — what's this!
MCCONOCHIE. Don't know sir.
BALL. Oh, yes, I think you do —
MCCONOCHIE. No —
BALL. In time of animals! You have had her!
MCCONOCHIE. Never!
BRADSHAW *(grabbing him).* Oh, I'll stick my dagger in your crack if you dirty doctor got in there before me!
MCCONOCHIE. Never! Never!

BALL. Dog-wise, yes, you did, I know it from your simper! *(MCCONOCHIE sobs.)* I never knew a doctor not share the sickbed of his patient had she got half a tit was healthy . . .
MCCONOCHIE. No . . . no . . .
BALL. *(his dagger out)*. Deny once more, I'll slit your carotids — there — I know a surgeon's patter — and see your gore across the shiny boards, I swear it! *(MCCONOCHIE freezes.)* So, was she hot for you? You being animal? Oh, was she, hot and clinging?
MCCONOCHIE. Yes . . .
BALL. And whispered you were wonder to her, being animal, sheer wonder, did she?
MCCONOCHIE. Yes . . .
BALL *(throwing him down)*. Oh, God and Christ, I do want a puritan woman! They know what they do with their eyes cast down and starchy collars! They do know it! 'Gone to be an animal!' Well, mistress, I shall find you in your den! *(He turns to go, stops.)* Can you cure me of what I've got? It stings me something awful.
MCCONOCHIE. I don't know what you —
BALL. I'll sit and unbutton. And if it rises thinking of the Bradshaw woman, tap it with some cold instrument. And blunt, mind you . . . *(He sits, unbuttons.* MCCONOCHIE *looks.)* Why are you snivelling? Am I so ill you cannot keep your tears back?
MCCONOCHIE. No, I . . .
BALL. Touch it, then, it won't bite you . . . *(*MCCONOCHIE *feigns an examination.)* I have been on my own soil for six months now, hounding communists and antichrists, doing the midnight knock on the doors of old republicans. It is my treat. I have been on an eight year holiday. How is it?
MCCONOCHIE. Mild, mild, I think . . .
BALL. Eight years, watching the cliffs of England from a whore's back on the continent, jostling Louis le this and Monsignor that, purple vicars and slag duchesses. I did not think I should get back, let alone rip down the lanes and burn the manors of this lot. How mild? No other quack could shift it.
MCCONOCHIE. Mild . . . and yet . . . tenacious . . .
BALL. Where's the sense in History? I came here to a feast of bonfire and applauding. Who would have flung shit in my eye once were all bow and scraping, and me with not a clean whole garment! I don't pretend to know no history. How is the knob, then? Can you cure him?
MCCONOCHIE *(bluffing)*. It is a somewhat rare infection . . .
BALL. Rare, is it? It would be.
MCCONOCHIE. Rare, definitely, rare, yes . . .

BALL. What became of all the roundhead troopers? Is their armour up behind the door? Or rusting in the cabbages? I seen none since I came here, prance in their cottages and get only silence, muddy silence, and they used to yell so much, chivvied the world's guts once — ow! Don't pluck it, quack, examine it!
MCCONOCHIE. I am very sorry . . . I am not a pox specialist . . .
BALL. What are you, then!
MCCONOCHIE *(shaking)*. It is not my speciality . . .
BALL. Listen quack, I get no fuck here, very well, but I shall have a cure for my trouble!
MCCONOCHIE. Yes —
BALL. Get down your pox book —
MCCONOCHIE. Yes —
BALL. And study it —
MCCONOCHIE. Yes —
BALL. Fast! In Jesus' name, I shall leave here healthy! *(*MCCONOCHIE *rises and hurries to the door.)* Quack! *(He stops.)* Listen. Now the puritans are done for you will make a living as a cock specialist, if you're so minded. We bring from Europe every boil and sore now, it's the restoration of old lewdness and the reign of fucking. Specialize in troubles of the mucus and you will live in posh, if posh you fancy. *(*MCCONOCHIE *perceives.)* Christ knows why I favour you like this. Do you angle after posh? I never knew a doctor didn't.
MCCONOCHIE. Yes.
BALL. Start here, then. On my ailing foreskin.

*Pause. Then filled with inspiration,*MCCONOCHIE *turns to leave. He stops at the door.*

MCCONOCHIE. Perhaps a little essence of saltpetre?
BALL. Why not? Fling the contents of the pharmacy at it.
MCCONOCHIE *(his mind racing)*. Or sulphur in suspension of boracic . . .
BALL. You mix, I'll do the swallowing.*(*MCCONOCHIE *leaves.)* And I spend the night here! Among her things, run my fingers through her garments, slip her knicker on my haunches and dream in her bed. Tomorrow I'll pursue her.

Scene Five

A field. A man digging, a woman watching, and a preacher.
FEAK. I done enough. Bring out the dead, Mrs.
EDGBASTON. In certain knowledge of thy resurrection, in confidence thy mouth will speak again, sleeping only till the call come, we plant thee like a seed to rise when anger warms the ground!
PYLE *(taking a rifle from a cloth).* Anybody looking?
FEAK. Give us it.
EDGBASTON. Oh, Lord of Battles, bless thy son, and keep his silence brief!
FEAK *(handling it fondly, offering the muzzle).* Give 'im a kiss, eh? *(PYLE kisses the muzzle.)* And you, Bob . . . *(EDGBASTON kisses it.)* Bye bye, pal . . .
EDGBASTON. Oh, death and mutilation to thy enemies! He shall return to us in blood and smoke, I vow!
FEAK. Where ain't I carted that bloody gun . . .
PYLE. Where ain't I cleaned it . . .
EDGBASTON. A crop of armour and a field of bullets from thy temper shall be harvested!
PYLE. Scotland, Ireland, Flanders, Jamaica . . .
FEAK. All for nothing.
PYLE. Good times . . .
FEAK. Ta ta, pal, it won't be Sue's fault you get dirt up yer spout now . . .
PYLE. Good times . . .
EDGBASTON. Oh, let his sleep be brief before our wrath return to boil, in blood and terror drive the stinking Stuart from our soil!
FEAK *(to* EDGBASTON*).* All right, Bob, you done? *(He nods.)* Cover it up, ducks. *(PYLE begins filling the grave.)* We was the champions. Now look at us. Time's a cunt.
PYLE. So's God.
EDGBASTON. Now, sister, you are letting your grief run away with you . . .
PYLE. Am I? I said he's a cunt, didn't I? He is a cunt.
EDGBASTON. And did He not guide the parliament to raise the standard of revolt? Did he not steer the Lord Protector in his —
PYLE. Oh, fuck the Protector, Bob . . .
EDGBASTON. I will not hear this scandal of Almighty God!

FEAK. Yer can't tell Sue, Bob, she's defaced too many monuments. Always first up cathedral aisles, our Sue, 'ammer flyin', trail a' broken glass an' angels' 'eads . . .
PYLE. Good times . . .
FEAK. Must end . . .
EDGBASTON. It is one thing to wreck the graven image, but another to attack His dwelling place inside our hearts.
PYLE *(patting down the eath with the flat of the shovel).* Show a bloke a good thing . . .

She notices BRADSHAW *and* SCROPE *are watching them. Pause.*

BRADSHAW. I must say I have some trouble following the Lord myself. His ways and so on. I expect we got too proud, don't you? He really has a passion about proudness. One day you're prancing and the next day you are in the trough. And vice versa, I expect, well, look at Charles Stuart, have you got a bun or something, we are starving. *(They look at her.)* Well, if not a bun, a —
FEAK. We are fuckin' ragbags as it is —
BRADSHAW. Yes, I can see that, I wasn't asking for your life-blood, only —
EDGBASTON. We live very frugal here —
BRADSHAW. Oh, come on, where's your charity?
PYLE. Charity's for comrades.
BRADSHAW. With all respect, I don't think you have quite grasped the principle of charity, have you? The point, I think, is that it's undiscriminating, am I right? *(She looks at* EDGBASTON. SCROPE *mutters to her.)*
SCROPE. Come on, we'll get nothing here —
BRADSHAW *(hissing).* **I want a bun.** *(She turns back to* EDGBASTON.*)* You're a preacher, aren't you? What is charity, isn't there a character of moral obligation in the word?
FEAK. You get none 'ere —
BRADSHAW *(turning on him).* **You get none 'ere!** Well, what does the meaning matter, the offence is clear enough **I see you kill the old republic here** and quite right, bury old equality, **who said that!** Shh! All these old dirty words, under the sod and stamp on them, come on — *(She turns to* SCROPE.*)*
EDGBASTON. We are wary of strangers —
BRADSHAW. No, no, don't be kind now, you will only suffer for it, keep your bun, a man must watch his bun nowadays, don't feed a stranger, what is this, the Commonwealth, **who said that,** not me!
SCROPE *(desperate).* Take it!
BRADSHAW. Shut up! We can have the lot off them! *(She turns back to*

them) I do respect your narrow eyes, your tight lip, very wise now, hands in pockets, there are bun thieves about! *(She makes as if to go.)*
FEAK.   What were you, Mrs? With the Republic? *(She stops, looks down at her garments.)*
BRADSHAW.   Do I look a duchess? My husband gave the king his death. Trembling somewhat. Well, wouldn't you? He expected God to strike him dead. Sat on a ring of rubber in case lightning struck his head.

Pause. Then PYLE *flings herself at* BRADSHAW's *feet and kisses her hand.*

FEAK.   Get buns!
BRADSHAW *(as* PYLE *hurries off).*   With butter!
FEAK.   An' beer!
BRADSHAW.   Two bottles!
FEAK.   Bring all the beer we got!
SCROPE *(in joy).*   Oh, Christ, I hurt with hunger!
EDGBASTON.   Our great rebels brought to this ... there is mud to your knees, sister ...
BRADSHAW.   So there is! You do see life without a carriage! Has she any bacon?
EDGBASTON *(shouting off).*   Bacon, sis!
FEAK.   We saw 'im, we was beside 'im when they axed the bugger Stuart, weren't us, Bob?
BRADSHAW.   Ask her to wrap a dinner up, in cloth or something —
EDGBASTON *(shouts).*   Make a dinner up! A dinner! Make one up!
FEAK.   Where you are standin', that's where we was, 12th Footguard, battle-dress in case a' bother, trailin' pikes —
EDGBASTON *(shouting).*   In a cloth! A dinner! Yes!
FEAK.   I said, that is the President a' Council, that is Bradshaw, 'e was like from 'ere to there — remember, Bob? An' 'e was pale, dead pale 'e was —
BRADSHAW.   He had a very fair skin —
FEAK.   Fuckin' right 'e did, an' when the blood spilt, did 'e jump!
EDGBASTON.   We all jumped —
FEAK.   I jumped, you jumped, every bugger jumped!
EDGBASTON.   **King's blood!**
FEAK.   An' I thought, Christ Almighty, it's the same as any other, it's the same red stuff ...
EDGBASTON.   Off came his shoe —
FEAK.   An' the foot —
EDGBASTON.   The foot without the shoe was going —
FEAK.   On the wooden boards —

EDGBASTON. Bang — bang —
FEAK. On this frosty mornin' —
EDGBASTON. Bang — bang, the Stuart foot . . .

PYLE *returns with a small parcel of food. They look at it disparagingly.*

FEAK. What's this?
PYLE. It's little. Because they gave us little.
EDGBASTON. Sue —
PYLE. You give what you get —
EDGBASTON. Sue —
PYLE. **Don't yer, though? That's life!** *(Pause.)* I thought, crossin' this field, this bloody field which is runnin' in our sweat an' our dad's sweat before us, what are yer doin', Sue, you silly bitch, why fetch for them?
BRADSHAW. Give us a bite.
PYLE. I thought, you are forgettin' something, girl, in your excitement you ain't thinking right.
BRADSHAW. Give us a bite.
PYLE. Because we came from 'ere, 'alf starved as usual out this bloody field to chuck the bastard Stuart over an' get Oliver an' Mr Bradshaw in, ten years of killin' Spaniards, Scots an' Irish, an' for what?
EDGBASTON. You are being most —
PYLE. To come back to this soddin' field again! This field of bloody clay, only this time it was buggered with the horses ridin' over it an' wouldn't take a crop —
FEAK. It was, Bob —
PYLE. But did they let us off the rent? Did they? I ask yer, did they give us one bloody little quarter off the rent?
FEAK. They never, Bob . . .
PYLE. An' we are still tryin' to wring a dinner out this mud! Commonwealth? Whose commonwealth? Give them dinner, I thought, fuck!

Pause. Then she holds out the food to BRADSHAW. *She takes it, sits at once and starts eating.* SCROPE *watches anxiously.*

SCROPE. I do think . . . with all respect . . . you are not being entirely fair . . . Mr Bradshaw . . . you may know . . . was highly critical . . . of the . . . slow progress . . . of agrarian . . . reform . . . the tenant question . . . very . . . memoranda . . . to . . . and . . . *(he drops to his knees and grabs at the food, stuffing it in his mouth in ecstasy.)* Oh! Oh! *(The others watch them a few moments, then drift off.* BRADSHAW *stops eating, stares after them.)*
BRADSHAW. Listen —
SCROPE. Mm — mmm —

BRADSHAW. Oh, listen. I did something.
SCROPE. Mm — mmm —
BRADSHAW. Will you listen to me.
SCROPE. Mm —
BRADSHAW. Scrope, I did it. When he kissed me. **I took his wallet.** Get on your feet!
SCROPE. Wha'?
BRADSHAW *(showing it).* **I took his wallet!** Oh, my lovely quick hands, look! *(He stares at her in horror.)* Congratulate me. *(He just stares.)* **Congratulate me, then.**
SCROPE. But they — they were our people —
BRADSHAW. **Congratulate me, then!** *(Pause. He stares at her.)*
SCROPE. You cannot do it to them . . .
BRADSHAW. I did, you see, I did!
SCROPE. Listen —
BRADSHAW. Look at my fingers! Aren't they wonderful, and swift? They tremble in their little ecstasy, do look!
SCROPE. Please, listen —
BRADSHAW *(collecting the remaining bread).* Hurry up, or they'll discover it, and then it's noses slit and ears off, do be quick!
SCROPE. I refuse to move until you hear me!
BRADSHAW *(stares).* What, then? What? *(Pause.)*
SCROPE. You must not injure people in their faith.
BRADSHAW. Why not? What's so precious about faith? Why can't it take a kicking like anything else? I do them a favour. They get an education, and I get a wallet. Cheap at the price, there is fuckall in it —
SCROPE. You swear, I hate to hear you —
BRADSHAW. Ask a rat about his faith! *(She starts to go.)*
SCROPE. Wait!
BRADSHAW. Scrope, your ears!
SCROPE. A man may be beaten, and his wife violated, and his house burned, and his children murdered by his enemies, and yet stay whole. But to be so treated by his friends . . . you encourage madness.
BRADSHAW. **I do know that.** Do you think I found it easy? It wasn't easy. But that's my triumph. Any fool can rob his enemy. Where's the victory in that?
SCROPE. Mr Bradshaw would suffer if he could see this . . .
BRADSHAW. It's a long time since he lost his eyes, if he ever had any. What colour were they? I forget . . . *(SCROPE begins to sob.)* Oh, Scrope, you are a wet little sparrow of a man . . .
FEAK *(off, distantly).* **Oi!**

SCROPE *(grabbing his satchel).* Oh, Christ!
BRADSHAW. Oh, Scrope, the argument...
FEAK. **Oi!**
BRADSHAW *(grinning as he tears offstage).* What about the argument?

Interlude

The vaults of the Bank of England. GAUKROGER *beats a staff.* HAMBRO *appears.*

GAUKROGER. Oh — King — Charles — our — rightful — chief!
HAMBRO. I am the Governor.
GAUKROGER. I am the Officer.
HAMBRO. Give me the keys.
GAUKROGER. What is the password?
HAMBRO. The password is orange.
GAUKROGER *(holds out a bunch of keys).* God save the monarch!
HAMBRO. His honour and his might! *(*GAUKROGER *marches out.)* Where are you, Frank? *(He jangles the keys.)* Oh, don't be a silly bugger.
MOBBERLEY *(from hiding).* 'is honour and 'is might...
HAMBRO. Quite.
MOBBERLEY. 'is bollocks and 'is conk...
HAMBRO. Very funny. Now, when you're ready, perhaps you'd help me get a table out.
MOBBERLEY *(stepping out the darkness).* Gimme the keys...
HAMBRO. Because I'm not doing this all by myself...
MOBBERLEY. Give us 'em.
HAMBRO *(shifting a table).* Frank, you are supposed to be the Minister for Public Works, I wish you'd —
MOBBERLEY. **I wanna look at me gold.**
HAMBRO. You can't. Bring over those chairs.
MOBBERLEY. **Show us me gold.**
HAMBRO. I keep trying to explain to you, it is not your gold, it's everybody's gold.
MOBBERLEY. **I wanna see my bit, then.**
HAMBRO *(pausing).* Frank, one of these days you will have to come to grips with the principles of banking —
MOBBERLEY *(snatching the keys).* **Got 'em! Ha, ha! Got 'em!**

HAMBRO. Sooner or later focus the great beams of your intellect on the mobility of money — *(He attempts to recover the keys.)* **Give them back.**
MOBBERLEY. **I don't trust yer!**
HAMBRO. This is precisely why we have a bank.
Pause. MOBBERLEY leans on the table.
MOBBERLEY. Billy, I am a brickman with paws so clumsy I can 'ardly scratch my name. All the juice in the royal 'ores' cunts will never make my fingers soft. I 'ad one kiln I fired with my own furniture, an' one cart, which when the army took the 'orse off me, I stood in the shafts myself. I now 'ave fifty carts an' fifty drivers, an' there ain't one night my wagon lights ain't bumpin' down the London road, come snow or flood. Show us me gold and don't fog my 'ead with science. *(He goes off to the vault. A man enters.)*
PARRY. I said velvet. Velvet, I said. Velvet, you silly arse. He thought the word was orange. I don't know about orange, I said, I only know velvet.
HAMBRO *(laying out glasses).* Velvet was last night.
PARRY. I will talk to Coldstream about his fucking guards. If he thought it was orange why did he let me in?
UNDY *(entering).* Oh, I love this place! I do love this place! I love its columns and its architraves, I love its Greekness! I could have been Romulus or Remus coming up them steps . . .
PARRY. They weren't Greeks, Ralph, they was Romans.
UNDY. The guard says 'what's the password?' Velvet, says I. No, he says, not velvet. It is fucking velvet, says I, if it's not velvet, what is it? Orange, he says —
PARRY. We have just been through this, Ralph.
UNDY. Oh, you have, have you?
PARRY. Where's Frank?
HAMBRO. Frank is in the vault.
PARRY. In the vault?
HAMBRO. He wants to — feel the ingots.
PARRY. Feel the ingots?
HAMBRO. Yes.
PARRY. **Feel the ingots?**
HAMBRO. That's what I said. I do think someone's got to talk to Frank.
UNDY. This is a palace you got here, Billy. The King will never have a better.
HAMBRO. No. He can't afford it, can he?
PARRY. Not on what we give him.
STREET and MONCRIEFF *(entering).* Are we late?
HAMBRO. Marginally.

STREET. I cannot stay late. I am in a slight hurry.
HAMBRO. We don't have much to discuss that concerns the Navy.
UNDY. What slight hurry is this, Stan? We have not met for three weeks, have we?
STREET. A masque in Putney.
UNDY *(disbelief)*. A masque in Putney?
STREET. My wife is expecting me.
UNDY. His wife is expecting him. Well, if his wife is expecting him, what's it matter we have not met in three weeks?
STREET. Don't be silly, Ralph.
UNDY. I'm surprised he could make it at all, what with his wife expecting him.
HAMBRO. Ralph...
UNDY. A most commanding lady is Joanna...
PARRY. Are we ready for the oath?
UNDY. We govern, and are governed in our turn, it seems, all our conference must hang on Stanley's wife. Does she know she governs the country, Stanley, may I ask?
HAMBRO. Ralph.
UNDY. I thought we had got rid of absolute monarchy, but no, there is Stanley's wife is more terrible than Louis le whatsname or the Tsar, kicking her heels in Putney, Christ help us —
PARRY. **The oath, Ralph!**
UNDY. Ludicrous.
HAMBRO. Please.
UNDY. It is.

They stand round the table, join hands over the bottle.

MONCRIEFF. Mobberley's not here.
PARRY. Fuck.
HAMBRO. F — R — A — N — K!
STREET. Leave him out of the oath.
UNDY. Can't.
HAMBRO. This once.
UNDY. Can't.
PARRY. As Stan's in a rush. Agreed?
UNDY. Bloody hell.
ALL. Agreed.
HAMBRO. Ralph?
UNDY. Stan's wife commandeth.

HAMBRO.   Go on, then, Bob.
PARRY *(reciting the oath).*   To those whom God grants power grant honour, equity and conscience too —
ALL.   Semper fidelis, Semper honorabilis, Semper, Semper —
UNDY.   Oh, Christ, what has Frank —
ALL.   Semper, Semper —
MOBBERLEY *(dragging some gold bars on a small trolley).*   **Got a bit of England, sir!**
PARRY.   Oh, put it back, Frank —
MOBBERLEY *(picking up a bar).*   In my grubby paw got boys and girls —
HAMBRO.   Just give us the keys —
MOBBERLEY.   **Got woods and fields and shops and rivers** —
HAMBRO.   Put them on the table, there's a good —
MOBBERLEY.   **An' fish an' fences, gardens, cradles, virgins, cots!**
HAMBRO.   Frank, I am the Governor of this place!
MONCRIEFF.   Leave him.
MOBBERLEY.   Leave me, Billy. I am hanging on to **my bit**. *(He sits at the empty chair.)* Did I miss anything?
UNDY.   You missed the oath.
MOBBERLEY *(putting the gold bar on his lap).*   Fuck the oath. *(He turns to his neighbour.)* I am keeping my gold indoors.
PARRY.   You can't.
MOBBELEY.   'oo says so?
PARRY.   You can't because we lend it to people.
MOBBERLEY.   I don't wanna lend it.
STREET.   You've got to. It's the system.
MOBBERLEY.   Who's system? Not my system!
UNDY.   I thought Frank was au fait with economics.
HAMBRO.   No . . .
UNDY.   Frank, I thought we had a civil war to get this straight. I spent four years on horseback chasing over garden fences to sort this out. Four years! And now you want to take your gold home and rip up the floorboards. **I have a wound five inches long in my groin says England's got to have a bank!** *(Pause.* MOBBERLEY *looks confused.)*
MOBBERLEY.   I keep getting bits of paper.
HAMBRO.   They are not bits of paper, they are credit notes . . .
MOBBERLEY.   It's still paper, ain't it?
HAMBRO.   **It's got my signature on!**
UNDY.   All right, Billy.
STREET.   I'm in a slight hurry, if you remember, so may I suggest —

MONCRIEFF *(paternally).* Hang aboot, hang aboot, will ye? Take your mind back to before the war. You may remember, before the war, the King told us to pay him money. Ordered us to, ye cud na argue with it. But we did na want to pay him money, so we had the war, all right? Now, we have a new King, an' he still wants money. He has to ha' the money from somewhere, it stands ta reason. But noo, instead o' givin' it to him, we lend it to him instead. Are ye clear on that, Frank? An' ye canna lend money if it's under the bed. *(He smiles.)* Now, goo an' put it back in the vaults, and when ye wanna see it, ye can see it, can't he, Billy, he can coom and look at his stuff. That's noo a lot to ask, is it?
HAMBRO. I suppose not.
MONCRIEFF. Of course he can. Okay? *(Pause.)*
MOBBERLEY. Sorry, I am being dense.
MONCRIEFF. Noo, noo, not at all. It's a complicated subject. Off ye goo.
*(*MOBBERLEY *gets up, tows his trolley away.)*
STREET. Now, can we get down to business? *(*HAMBRO *rises to his feet.)*
HAMBRO. I want to stop the terror.
PARRY. Why?
HAMBRO. Well, why not?
UNDY. Yes, why not, Bob? I think we've had enough of randy cavaliers knocking the eyeballs out of puritans. It's all right for a fortnight, but I had a Dutchman lose an ear last week and he was here to place a contract.
PARRY. They must have their fling.
UNDY. I think they've had it. Christ, all the republicans are still in hiding.
PARRY. No. Let 'em rampage a while yet, or they will turn their attention elsewhere. Let 'em beat the communists, and the pamphlet writers and the free love and the Christ-on-earth mob, let 'em carve the king's initials on their arses.
UNDY. I would be perfectly happy for that, but they are getting indiscriminate.
HAMBRO. They are getting out of hand, Bob.
PARRY. They are meant to be out of hand, they are cavaliers, aren't they? They have been rotting in foreign brothels for ten years, they are bound to be out of hand.
UNDY. They are blinding my customers.
PARRY. All right, and what do you intend to do with them?
HAMBRO. Enlist them in a regiment. Give them a uniform with lots of tassel and gold facing. Call them The King's Own and send them on an expedition from which they won't come back.
PARRY. They are too old for expeditions. They are antiquated thugs who lost their estates for monarchy and if we don't let 'em rollock they will sit about on doorsteps and start to think —

UNDY. What with, Bob?
PARRY. And they will think —
UNDY. What with, exactly?
PARRY. With what is left of their brains —
UNDY. Never had any —
PARRY. Whatever happened to their little estates, and they will look around and they will see who has 'em —
UNDY. Never —
PARRY. And it will be us —
UNDY. Oh, bollocks, Bob —
PARRY. And we will be in deep shit I tell you.
HAMBRO. Bob, you are governing England now. I do think, when a man is governing England, he oughtn't to shudder so much.
UNDY. 'ear, 'ear!
HAMBRO. No one will undo the settlement. Let them rot in taverns and piss their grievances down the sink.
UNDY. 'ear, 'ear!
STREET. Shall we vote?
UNDY. Why not? Stan's in a hurry, mustn't forget.
HAMBRO. Those in favour of calling them off? *(A majority of hands are raised.)* It's off.
CHARLES *(off)*. **Orange, he quoth!**
UNDY *(jumping up)*. Fuck, it's the mad shagman!
HAMBRO *(clearing the desk)*. Look casual!
MOBBERLEY *(entering)*. I put 'em back —
UNDY. Siddown!
HAMBRO. It's a drink — it's only a drink!
CHARLES *(entering)*. **Not enter my bank!**
GAUKROGER. Did not know you, sir!
CHARLES. Did not know me! And have I not the conk? The conk which goes before me crying **Monarch?** Orange or velvet, here's the conk! *(He thrusts his face at* GAUKROGER, *catches sight of the bankers.)* Oh, there's a do! There's a do in my bank!
HAMBRO *(bowing)*. Sir, a glass?
NODD *(entering)*. 'ullo, Billy, workin' late?
CHARLES. An' Undy, an' Mobb'ley, what's this?
GWYNN *(entering)*. Men only.
CHARLES. Come to show Nelly me bank, an' there's a beano!
HAMBRO. A seat, madam?
GWYNN. No, give us the keys.
CHARLES *(peering)*. An' Parry! Well, fuck me, what's this?

PARRY. Well, wc meet . . .
CHARLES. Oh, yer meet, do yer? An' who's that?
NODD. Dunno, 'o is it? *(STREET bows.)*
CHARLES. Oh, Stanley, you too?
NODD. 'o is 'e? Somethin' legal ain't 'e?
CHARLES. Something legal, he says. He is Chief Justice, yer ass. Well, I'm buggered at this . . . *(He sits in a chair.)*
GWYNN. Where's the gold, Charlie?
CHARLES. Give her the keys.
HAMBRO *(taking them off the table).* There are three doors to the vault, each one with an eight-lever lock —
CHARLES. Don't blind her with science, she is after rubbing her bosoms over the bricks.
GWYNN *(taking the keys).* Can I 'ave one?
HAMBRO. Can you have one?
GWYNN. A gold brick. *(Pause. She looks at* CHARLES.*)*
NODD. Go on, give 'er one. *(Pause.)*
HAMBRO. I should like nothing more, only —
NODD. No, no, stuff all that. Give 'er one.
HAMBRO. It isn't that simple.
CHARLES. Why ain't it?
HAMBRO. Each brick represents —
CHARLES. Respresents what?
HAMBRO. The accumulation of other men's wealth.
NODD. Well, that's why she wants it. She ain't a nana. Give 'er one, then.

HAMBRO *looks resolutely at the floor.*

GWYNN. Oh, Charlie, 'e don't want to! *(He looks at him.)* Ain't you mean, when you got such a lot?
NODD. Take it. G'arn take it. *(Pause.* CHARLES *gets up.)*
CHARLES. I may not. Do you see, Noddy? I may not.
NODD *(to* GAUKROGER*).* Oi, you! You git down there an' bring us a brick!*(*GAUKROGER *looks at* HAMBRO.*)* Look smart, then! *(He doesn't move.)*
CHARLES. No, I may not . . . *(He moves away.)*
NODD. Oh, you crew of fuckers —
CHARLES. Nodd —
NODD. What's yer racket, eh? Down 'ere in the dead a' night, what is it?
CHARLES. Nodd —
NODD. It's a conspiracy, ain't it? When two or three are gathered together, charge 'em, it's treason an' you know it —

CHARLES. Nodd, you will make enemies of powerful men —
NODD. Fucked if I care —
CHARLES. I can't save you. Even my dad — my dad who was absolute and had God sitting in his eyeballs — could not save his pals, his bumloves and his vicars — they look at you so darkly, Nodd, take a warning from their looks! *(He goes up to them mockingly.)* Oh, do not hurt my Noddy, he is a slumboy, all cock and prattle, do not murder him, you will make all Southwark weep . . .
UNDY. His Majesty has had a long evening . . .
CHARLES. He thinks I'm tired —
UNDY. Perhaps a carriage —
CHARLES. No, Ralph, you are too kind, you are too generous, he offers me a carriage, such a nice, nice man . . . I do like Ralph . . . *(He turns to go, stops.)* What are you doing down here? *(They are silent.)* Well, I can't bring charges, the chief lawyer's here himself!
NODD. Turn the mob out!
CHARLES. The mob — the mob — his touching adulation of the mob —
NODD. My mates —
CHARLES. Oh, Christ, spare us your mates —
NODD. Give over —
CHARLES. He thinks to terrorize you with his mates, the legion of the half cut, frighten Ralph, don't it touch you, Ralph, with its naivety?
NODD. All right, fuck yourself —
CHARLES. Mobs, no, **show 'em the look that stops their hearts!** *(He leans on the table, intimately.)* You will like this, I know you will, and you Billy, you will love this — *(He turns to* NODD, *who is feeling in a bag.)* **Hurry up, we're waiting!** Give it to Nell, she can handle flesh, Nell, show the gentlemen the way you kiss, there is no kissing like her, you would think all the kissin' I done there was nothing left to be discovered, but there is, there is! *(*GWYNN *takes the head of* BRADSHAW *from* NODD *and holding it in both hands, kisses the mouth.)* Watch her lip now! Can yer see, Ralph? Do come nearer, and you, Mobberley, she has a kiss as long as the coast, oh, she makes yer faint, she does! *(He goes close to* HAMBRO.*)* Was he ever done like that, I ask yer, Billy, was he, do yer think?
HAMBRO. I don't know who kissed him.
CHARLES. Oh, Billy don't remember who lipped him, Robert, you would know! *(*PARRY *shakes his head.)* Nobody? And you were peas once in the pod of the Republic! Oh, look at his one eye, the single eyeball does look sad to be rejected, his one eye that says **long cold nights of serious thought.** Scaring, ain't it, Mobb'ley. **The man who thinks us to death!** Show Ralph!
UNDY *(as* GWYNN *moves near him.)* 'ullo, Dick, 'ow are yer?

CHARLES. Oh, now, wit! Ralph's mordant wit! Look him in the eye, Ralph, the eye please, fix it . . .
UNDY *(looking).* Been having late nights again, old son . . .
CHARLES. **No, look at him!**
UNDY. I am looking at him.
CHARLES. I hear he never slept.
UNDY. Well, you can see that.
CHARLES. But worked all nights.
UNDY. So they tell me.
CHARLES. Planning new commonwealths.
UNDY. Very likely . . .
CHARLES. Ever more common. Ever less wealthy.
UNDY. He 'ad some funny ideas . . .
CHARLES. Writing constitutions in the starry night, while moths struck the window . . .
UNDY. Quite . . .
CHARLES. While the rain lashed, plotted the extinction of private property . . .
UNDY. Wouldn't put it past 'im . . .
CHARLES. **Plotted the extinction of you, Ralph!***(He leans closer, quoting from the 'Harmonia Britannia'.)* 'And there were some called rich, who gathered to themselves the labour and the inventiveness of others, and kept them brutally in place, but these were like a nightmare or bad memory, for in Harmonia there was neither gold nor money, but such things were laughed at as a superstition and a dead weight in the pocket . . . ' There, I know my Bradshaw, banned book but I got him in my library . . . *(He tilts the head up and down.)* Word perfect, ain't I? Yes, he says . . . *(He tosses the head to NODD.)* Stick him back in the bag, he makes their bowels go loose, or Ralph all witty, which is the same thing, same stink, ain't it? Nell, wish the gents goodnight . . .
GWYNN. Ta ta —
HAMBRO *(arising, bowing).* Sire, good night —
CHARLES. Down poodles, down spaniels!
NODD. Woof, woof!
GWYNN. Ol' buggers, aincha?
CHARLES *(to* GAUKROGER*).* Orange or velvet?
GAUKROGER. Whatever you say, Sire —
CHARLES. Oh, you are too accommodating! And me only a monarch too!

They go out. HAMBRO *etc remain standing, silently. Pause.*
UNDY. Billy . . .
HAMBRO. I know . . .
UNDY. No, let me say this —
HAMBRO. I know what you're going to say —
UNDY. I still wanna say it —
HAMBRO. If you must —
UNDY. I must. **Why in Christ's name did we bring that back?**
PARRY. Have a drink, Ralph —
UNDY. Fuck the drink —
PARRY *(offering* MONCRIEFF*).* Andrew?
UNDY. **Why**
HAMBRO. I think you know why.
UNDY.   **Out — fucking — rageous!**
STREET. Sit down, Ralph . . .
UNDY. **Impert — inence!**
HAMBRO. Ralph, he knows. And that is all that matters.
UNDY. I got my pride!
HAMBRO. **He knows.** *(Pause.)* The rest is shrill and squealing. Never mind the squeal. I don't.

ACT TWO

Scene One

Beside the Thames in Essex. DEVONSHIRE *in a cloak, looks out. At a distance, a* FOOTMAN.

DEVONSHIRE. I do feel clean here. I do feel clean. The wind off the estuary. The cockle-women shouting I can't hear. And the low cloud racing, and the grey flat water, the thin surf on the mudbank, really it is better than a marine landscape by Mr Van Oots and in any case I don't think I like sex. *(Pause. She breathes.)* Oh, this is pure, this is absolute life, I never felt so whole and so completely independent, this is the third letter in a week begging me back and in verse too! All very flattering but really it is pure dick, a woman should never forget a poem is actually dick, should she? I don't believe before Mr Van Oots anyone went near a beach, you can't smell the seaweed in a painting, can you?

FOOTMAN. **Oi, get back!**

BEGGARS *(throwing themselves before her).* Alms, miss!

DEVONSHIRE. Or the beggars, for that matter . . .

FOOTMAN *(wading in among them).* Fuck off!

DEVONSHIRE. You are in pain, I know you are, you don't have to tell me, and I tell you that I am too! Does that sound callous? *(They look at her. She goes towards them.)* To look at me you'd think she knows no pain, now, wouldn't you? I'm sure you say that, privately. Admit you say that.

BEGGARS. No —

DEVONSHIRE. Oh, you do, you do! Her lovely this, her lovely that, compared to us in our rags and shanties, you do, of course you do, you think I have no agonies. But there are pains and pains, aren't there? *(They look blank.)* No? *(They look blank.)* Pains of the mind?

BRADSHAW. Yes.

DEVONSHIRE. Somebody knows! And they are, if anything, worse than the pains of hunger or whatever you are on about, because there is no cure. No, no cure! I have a pain like that. Believe me. Now, hurry off before Sam

gets awful — *(She dips in a purse and throws small change about.)* . . . and think of me sometimes, and see the pain is not all on your side, mm?
FOOTMAN.   All right, scarper!
BRADSHAW *(not moving).*   Tell you about your pain.
FOOTMAN.   Fuck off, I said —
BRADSHAW.   Go on, let me —
FOOTMAN *(to her face).*   **Oi!**
DEVONSHIRE *(turning away).*   Don't kick her. I don't own the beach.
FOOTMAN.   Above the tidemark —
DEVONSHIRE.   Oh, sod that — *(Pause.* FOOTMAN *stands away.)*
BRADSHAW.   All my knowledge. Give it to you. All my life.
DEVONSHIRE.   Why?
BRADSHAW.   Because you're shallow.
DEVONSHIRE.   Oh, I am, am I?
BRADSHAW.   And a bit cruel with it.
DEVONSHIRE.   Do watch it dear, Sam will kick you in the head.
BRADSHAW.   Yes. *(Pause.)*
DEVONSHIRE.   This is my beach and so is everything else that you can see. I am twenty-four and have miscarried seven times. That is wicked, isn't it, of God? Have you miscarried?
BRADSHAW.   Yes.
DEVONSHIRE.   It is particularly cruel because I care for men. Last week I thought the floor of my body was being bitten out, by rats, by dogs, I thought my whole floor going, have you had that?
BRADSHAW.   Yes.
DEVONSHIRE.   I cannot keep a child in, absolutely cannot, yet I conceive from a look, what is the matter with God, my womb is only fit for a nun, or is He trying to tell me to be a nun, is that His way, do you think? I will die from one of these drops. I would keep away from dick if I could, but you cannot be as good as I am, looking as I do, and keep away from them, can you? I am trying to appreciate views instead, but he writes so beautifully, my rump, my rump, he goes on about, keeps him awake at nights, my whispering hair and so on, I go back tonight, I know all poems are dick but I go back, I will die of him, it is silly but he makes me feel alive. What's your advice? I believe in asking strangers for advice, you cannot trust your friends. I believe in essence all your friends wish you dead. Say yes or no.
BRADSHAW.   Yes.
DEVONSHIRE *(turning on her).*   You only want to get me killed! *(Pause.)* Really, what kind of advice is that? Forty years old, are you, and you say one syllable. Get off my beach. Sam . . . *(She goes to leave.)*

BRADSHAW. How dare you turn your back, I have given you the education of a lifetime!
DEVONSHIRE. All you said was yes.
BRADSHAW. Yes was all you asked for.
DEVONSHIRE. I'm not to be taken literally.
BRADSHAW. I will tell you what yes means, shall I? *(Pause.)* Shall I?
DEVONSHIRE. Go on.
BRADSHAW. Yes means no resistance. Yes means going with the current. Yes means lying down when it rains and standing up when it's sunny. Yes urge. Yes womb. Yes power. I lived with a man whose no was in the middle of his heart, whose no kept him thin as a bone and stole the juices from him. No is pain and yes is pleasure, no is man and yes is nature. Yes is old age and no is early death. Yes is laughter, no is torture. I hate no. No is misery and lonely nights. Do you follow or shall I say it again?

Pause. Then DEVONSHIRE unclasps her cloak and lays it over BRADSHAW's shoulders.

DEVONSHIRE. Take all the cockles off the beach. *(She turns to go.)*
BRADSHAW. Let me be your servant.
DEVONSHIRE. I don't need a servant.
BRADSHAW *(crawling to her feet)*. I will give you service of my life's blood though you are the worst bitch in the kingdom and pay me never. Employ me. I'll turn the kitchen spit with my teeth.
DEVONSHIRE. And you think me shallow?
BRADSHAW. Perfection. *(Pause. She looks at FOOTMAN, who shakes his head. She smiles.)*
DEVONSHIRE. I live in Blackfriars.

She goes out, followed by FOOTMAN, who is barely offstage when he turns and runs back.

FOOTMAN. You're no skivvy! I seen you! All you old republicans, six months ago you wouldn't call no geezer master, now look at yer! **I'm the true skivvy! You will kill the trade you bleeders!** Coming! *(He runs off again. BRADSHAW is on her knees when SCROPE enters.)*
SCROPE. I do not, of the obscene career I've witnessed, care to specify which gave me the most horror, watching old women cheated from behind a bush, or in this instance tucked behind a dune, seeing you fondling the foot of the most callous whore to flounce in daft courts. **Take off that purple badge of shame, please** ... I do believe I saw Mr Bradshaw thin and gaunt with pain creep over the water ... his kind eyes in the candlelight while we planned constitutions and just wars ...

BRADSHAW.   Have a cockle . . .
SCROPE.   I believe no woman came nearer to touching saintliness than you and you — do not eat with your mouth open, I do hate that doglike manner!
BRADSHAW *(opening the cloak).*   Come under with me, there's a cruel wind off the water . . .
SCROPE.   I was thinking today just where his greatness lay, and it lay in this, that nothing was ever set firmly in his mind, but he would challenge every thought and beat it round his head like a bear set on by dogs, stagger it from corner into corner, was it good, was it proper, the bloody bear pit of his mind! *(He sits beside* BRADSHAW. *She covers him.)* And me . . . it is my misfortune to have served him, who blew out my little candle with his great light . . . when I might have written . . . might have . . . **Lost my chance now!** *(He begins to sob.)*
BRADSHAW.   Oh, don't cry for Christ's sake —
SCROPE.   I have to! I'm not ashamed of tears!
BRADSHAW.   You only cry because you want to impress me.
SCROPE.   Rubbish.
BRADSHAW.   You do. To show how great your soul is. From now on I am banning crying. You've been snivelling on and off since Norwich.
SCROPE.   I've not . . .!
BRADSHAW.   A red eye in the wind, some wail coming out the hay at night. Tears are a rebuke, to man or nature. Protests, aren't they? I don't protest, and I'll be happy. See if I ever cry again.

Suddenly BALL *bursts out of cover, waving a sword.*

BALL.   You never paid your drink in Roxworth! Took the ale and scarpered! Oh, trail of scrounging and cruel little knocks, **I am entitled to punish in the name of the Stuart. Get over there you!**
SCROPE.   Oh God . . .!
BALL.   **Over or I cut yer!** *(*SCROPE *rolls into a ball, away from* BRADSHAW.*)* I have hunted you from your bed madam, from the smell of your sheets I have, show me your face, your thin, dry lips, show me, you may not leave your domicile if you were of the rule of anti-Christ the Commonwealth, you broke the regulation, did you think I'd let my fancy go? **I am come into my rights!** *(He swings to* SCROPE.*)* Stay there you ball of scrawn and bollock **I am the governor now!** *(He turns back to* BRADSHAW.*)* Listen, I have been drinking and not paying either, but I may do 'cos I suffered, no publican gives me a cacky look I bust his lip for him, I have been drinking and I love you, stand up, it offends me to see a woman crouching, is he to do with you? What is he? Be my darling, I have a thing about you, you

could be as rough as fifty hellbags, I still got a thing for you, I don't know what my passion's coming to, to be honest you are nothing to stare after, why am I fixed like this?

BRADSHAW. It happens.

BALL. Fuck, it does, and I shall love you on this shore, or stab you, I am that bewildered! Let me worship, God, your eyes are tired and yet full of secrets, I wrote you a poem, no, I tell a lie, I wrote thirty, thirty sonnets in one night, there is cavalier art for you, I was up to dawn and squinting by a candle in the guest-room of some inn, 'sir, your boots on the boards keep us awake' cries the publican, 'balls to your kip,' says I, 'I am creating, I am sonnet mad for Bradshaw!' Read this one, or shall I? *(He takes a paper from his pocket.)* This is the best, this is the cream, in the Italian manner, I should bawl it in palazzios but this stinking beach will do it, shall you read it or shall I?

BRADSHAW. You.

BALL. I am a poor reader —

BRADSHAW. Oh, don't say that —

BALL. All right — *(He swings back to* SCROPE.*)* **Don't shift or I'll split your liver!** *(He turns back.)* It goes, I start — Christ, this beach stinks — I call it — 'A Love Unexpected' — it is twelve lines in the Tuscan manner — **I don't think I can do it justice** — notwithstanding that, I — I — it — *(He lets his hand droop.)* I will fuck you or I shall go mad. You have given me hell these last ten nights.

BRADSHAW. The poem.

BALL. No, no —

BRADSHAW. Perhaps I —

BALL. No, no, the poem, stuff it — *(He thrusts it back in his pocket.)* There is a hut over there, go into it —

BRADSHAW. You are going to force me —

BALL. Yes. Quick now.

BRADSHAW. I prefer you read the poem —

BALL. **Look, I am an agent of Charles Stuart, all I do is legal, naught is wrong, see?** *(Pause.)* I worship, I bring my poor love to the altar, over there out the wind now . . .

BRADSHAW. God help me to do this . . .

BALL. He will, Christ knows you are perfect to me . . .

She seems to prepare herself, then goes out. BALL *looks round quickly, then follows her.* SCROPE *staring, quotes from the 'Harmonia Britannia'.*

SCROPE. 'And there will be love betwixt man and woman of a sort not known yet, founded on freedom of will and desire, so that she shall not be hampered by false modesty nor him by his cult manliness . . .' *(He shudders with a paroxysm of impotent anger.)* Oh, all you who come after, make your revolution right! *(He takes the book from his pocket and flings it into the mud, weeps. Pause.* BALL *returns.)*

BALL. It is a funny thing this, and I have never found it otherwise, that I come off so miserable I could weep or join a priesthood. I am off to fish in some pond, have an awful need for some tranquility . . . *(He goes a little way, stops, holds out the poem.)* Will you give her this? I think love would be to come off and be happy . . .

SCROPE *takes the poem.* BALL *walks off. After a pause,* BRADSHAW *returns, by a great effort of will she resumes exactly the posture she occupied before his arrival. Pause.*

BRADSHAW. You know, do you, for seven years Bradshaw did not come near me?

SCROPE. How should I know?

BRADSHAW. Well, I tell you. Could not come near me for the power of his thought, his nightmare. So I was untouched.

SCROPE. Oh.

BRADSHAW. So this one licked me. *(*SCROPE *turns away.)* **Licked me and opened me again.** *(Pause.)* And I —

SCROPE. Go, shall we?

BRADSHAW. Felt sorry that he left me so depressed . . . *(Long pause.)*

SCROPE *(bitterly).* You seem — you take this — very — Oh, I don't know, cowlike, stand up to nothing now, but bend down and so on, no tears or protest, wisdom of compliance and so on, but — well, I — *(He faces her.)* Suppose I — what if I —

BRADSHAW *(seeing the direction).* Scrope, I don't wish it —

SCROPE. Wish it? What's this wish it? What are wishes, what are tears?

BRADSHAW. I don't —

SCROPE. You don't? And how do you know I have not also found you beautiful? What of my compulsion? I have slept beside you on trestles and on bales in barns and never once out of respect for him —

BRADSHAW. Him?

SCROPE. Him who was my master, yes, out of respect not once lifted my hand to you, yet any coloured, drunken royalist can take you and —

BRADSHAW. Oh, God . . .

SCROPE. And you regret he did not feel a pleasure! What of me, I have the same thing, don't I —

BRADSHAW. I saw you as a friend, I —

SCROPE. No friend, never! I am a man, too! *(Pause.)*
BRADSHAW. I could not keep him off. You I can easily push over . . .
SCROPE. **Well, where's the justice in that!**
BRADSHAW *(standing up to go).* Don't know the word . . .
SCROPE *(grabbing her roughly).* Do it with me, now —
BRADSHAW. Look —
SCROPE. **Must! Must!**
BRADSHAW. You'll only hate me for it —
SCROPE. No —
BRADSHAW. What about your honour —
SCROPE. Never mind it —
BRADSHAW. You know what you'll be like, don't you, it'll be recrimination and —
SCROPE. **Never mind it, I said, never mind!** *(Pause. She turns to him. He buries his face in her breasts.)* Oh, my love, oh!

Scene Two

A garden in London. MILTON *is staring blindly at a rose.* CLEGG *is watching him, with* SCROPE.

CLEGG. I hide Mr Milton in my garden, though the penalty for concealing him is death, and me, who is court poet, double death of some description. I do this for literature, though I hate his views, though his politics offend me and his poetry upset my gut, I do it in case one day he writes a good thing in adversity. I am a very decent man, especially since I am so minor I will be forgotten quicker than my eyes melt into muck and no one prints my plays. I could happily denounce him out of envy, but I don't, Mr Milton always knew how to cultivate his enemies, didn't you, John, in case the Commonwealth collapsed? He doesn't answer, but then he is chock-a-block with cunning. This is Mr Scrope, who is educated, persecuted, and all the rest. He won't answer yet. *(Pause. They wander.)* I am a King's man, and a property man, and a Bishops' man, and everything John hates man, yet I hide him in my roses, I do believe I am the best that England makes, and have tolerance, which is more than John does. I am the author of a tragedy, 'Mayhem in Attica', in which the moral strength of the nation is shown to be inseparably linked to its respect for property. I have shown this to John, who says the Commonwealth was not opposed to property, on the contrary, John has a little bit himself. It is a fine play, but I warrant will be unknown to posterity, unlike John's stuff. I shall be buried in some obscure grave and no one will traipse to visit me, I don't know why I save him from execution, I must be mad, but you see I have my envy under firm control, it was envy brought the civil war on, though John calls it justice, no, it was envy and it could not last . . .
SCROPE. I'm afraid I am not acquainted with your work, Mr Clegg . . .
CLEGG. What a surprise! He has not heard of me! You hear that, John?
SCROPE. I have heard of you —
CLEGG. He **has** heard of me! Well, more surprising still, I am heard of! Forget the name, don't waste a useful space inside your memory for such a mediocre talent, there is Mr Milton there —
SCROPE. Of course I know Mr Milton —
CLEGG. Oh, you do, do you? Well, fancy, heard of Mr Milton, John, your luck is in! How well do you know my plays?
SCROPE. I am not a play-going man —

CLEGG. Well, no surprise, there has been a slight dearth of theatre the last twenty years! You shall see 'Mayhem in Attica', I have been promised a production, I cannot say when, but the promise is there, for what a promise is worth, not a lot in the theatre, I assure you, but it exists. *(He grins at* SCROPE.*)* No, I tease you, don't waste your time on a man whose statue there is no subscription for, dogs will shit on my grave and lovers grapple on it, and none will say 'Here lies Clegg who spared Milton and had a mediocre talent.' No, stay at home and read John. Do you care for roses?
SCROPE. Yes.
CLEGG. I hope I shall not be sent any more of you atheistic wretches to shelter, I am a King's man after all and fought your lot at Worcester, cut a man's arm off and nearly fainted, where were you?
SCROPE. I was at no battles.
CLEGG. No more was John, but then you do well with a pamphlet, do you?
SCROPE. I was Secretary to the Council . . .
CLEGG. Oh, and took down all their evil in a book! I have a garden full of enemies! Am I not the best of men? I dread to think the boot were on the other foot, you would put my eyes out. Want a cordial, John? Look, I wait on him and yet I hate his views. *(He goes out to fetch drinks.* SCROPE *nervously advances to* MILTON, *stops, hesitates.)*
SCROPE. I wonder, sir, if you feel able to elucidate us . . . as to the failure of our struggle . . . *(He ignores this.)* The errors in our calculation and —
MILTON. Shit and God. *(Pause.)*
SCROPE. Yes?
MILTON. Man.
SCROPE. Yes?
MILTON. **Shit and God.** *(*BRADSHAW *enters.)*
BRADSHAW. I had forgot the peeing you do with a child —
SCROPE. Shh!
BRADSHAW. What?
SCROPE. This is Milton.
BRADSHAW. Don't he know a woman pisses?
SCROPE. **No, he doesn't. Please shut up.**
BRADSHAW. He must do, didn't he go to bed with one?
SCROPE. **I beg you don't embarrass me.** *(Pause. She goes to* MILTON, *who has not moved.)*
BRADSHAW. I had a husband sat by you, and hatched a thing or two together, 'De Rerum Magisterium' or something, you would know Latin, on our lawn one summer, side by side in deckchairs with cloud scudding over Suffolk, in the sunshine writing revolution, now I kip in barns or gutters,

there's a turn-up for you, your name is a good excuse for knifing and my old man's hanging on Blackfriars, oh, don't look so tragic, you are all right, they don't kill poets —
SCROPE.   Our primary task must be — in my estimation — the examination of our errors —
BRADSHAW.   Bradshaw left his bed in dead of night — did you do this — grappling for a pencil — mutter, mutter — kicks the pisspot over — wakes the house —
SCROPE.   All is not wasted if error can be the educator of the future —
BRADSHAW.   Night after night this — I said for all the warmth you bring, you might sleep in your study — and dropped his linen everywhere — are you like that — found items of his underwear on stairs — shitty drawers he could not bring himself to part with —
SCROPE.   This is not true —
BRADSHAW.   And scratching! You never saw a barmy cat more vicious with itself, could bleed sometimes from some raw eczema itch — here — behind the ear — look — mad fingers — **are you watching!**
SCROPE.   **This is John Milton, you bitch.** *(Pause. She looks at Milton.)*
BRADSHAW.   Put your fingers on me. Read my face. I'm not the woman I was, am I? Tell me I'm not! *(He does not move.)* Thank you. *(Pause. She looks at him.)* I do think it's impossible to respect a genius when he's out of luck. I do. I quailed before you once, couldn't bring myself to speak — not that Bradshaw wanted me to, did he — just cart the sandwiches this way and that — but really, you made me tremble, and now you move me so little I could — *(with a sudden inspiration, she slaps his face.)*
MILTON.   **Aaaggghhh!**
CLEGG *(returning with a tray).*   Oh, don't do that . . .
MILTON.   **Aaaggghhh!**
SCROPE *(to* BRADSHAW*).*   **I hate you for that!**
BRADSHAW *(in delight).*   No, look —
SCROPE.   **Hate you for that!**
BRADSHAW.   See what I did!
SCROPE.   **Ugly! Ugly!**
MILTON.   **Aaaggghhh!**
CLEGG.   I always said, you need not fight the rebels, just lock them in a chamber and they will die of arguing within a week —
SCROPE.   **Ugly! Ugly!**
CLEGG.   Have a cordial . . .
BRADSHAW *(going to* MILTON*).*   Oh, don't cry. I didn't hurt you —
SCROPE.   **Hurt she says!**

BRADSHAW *(turning to him).* I didn't! *(And to* MILTON.*)* Listen, if you knew how it mattered I could do that! You don't, do you? You have no idea! I feel so grateful I could slap you again! *(To* SCROPE.*)* **Don't worry I shan't!** *(To* MILTON.*)* Try to understand me. I have broken myself into pieces to do this . . .
MILTON. I do not like women.
BRADSHAW. No, of course . . . *(Pause. She looks at* CLEGG.*)* Find Scrope some little task. He will copy out your Latin, and feel his honour is all safe. And when the shout dies down, get him in some college —
SCROPE. **Do not dare to intercede for me!** *(Pause. She turns to him.)*
BRADSHAW. Good bye. *(She holds out a hand.)*
SCROPE. I will not shake your hand.
BRADSHAW *(fondly).* Oh, my little lover —
SCROPE. **Do not say that, please!** *(Pause. She goes out.)*
MILTON. She slapped my face because her heart is broken. I find that comprehensible. When the war is won, wage war on the victors. Every civil war must be the parent of another. Those given laurels praise then execute. And their executioners, when the time comes, execute them too. Any amount of war a man will take, will acquiesce in his own destruction even, provided that he knows the change takes place. That is the God in him. But if after the first war, you only heap praise on the victors, they will make themselves your masters, even ape the first oppressor and invite him back. Any amount of power a man will take, provided we permit it. That is the shit in him. Next time, should we start there must be no finish, or we shall slap one another's faces in the gardens of our enemies . . .

Fade to black.

Scene Three

A gate in Blackfriars. BRADSHAW *is looking up at something black and shapeless on a spike. Long pause. She conquers herself.*

BRADSHAW. I was deceived. Bradshaw was an African. I never stripped in daylight, nor him either. How was I to know he was an African? **No wonder we had revolution, the moors had got into our beds.** I can't think why there's flesh on it, the birds here are so finicky. **What's the matter, isn't the meat good enough for you?** *(A soldier appears.)* That is perfectly good man, you fussy buggers!
SHADE. Now, then.
BRADSHAW. Why is he black?
SHADE. Sunshine, ain't it?
BRADSHAW. It's a bit well done for me, but never mind, I can find a use for it, get it down, ducks.
SHADE. You wouldn't be the fuss to ask . . .
BRADSHAW. Well, no, there is a wicked shortage of cagmag, isn't there? People will use anything to make a stew. And they call this a restoration! A restoration of what, starvation? **Who said that!** *(She pretends to look behind her.)* Come on, give us it, he was my husband.
SHADE. And I'm Father Christmas.
BRADSHAW. What do you expect, the cock to rise? Look, I have the other quarters in the bag — *(She opens a large bag.)*
SHADE. Oh, fuckin' 'ell . . .
BRADSHAW. Nip up and get it, there's a love. They were so good to me at Moorgate, they even wrapped it up, like butchers —
SHADE *(moving her on).* Come on, darling, get along —
BRADSHAW. Don't hustle me —
SHADE. Move, then —
BRADSHAW. Who owns the pavement —
SHADE. I do —
BRADSHAW. Get it for me — listen — **Who are you shoving — will somebody witness this!**
SHADE. You barmy bitch —
BRADSHAW. **Somebody witness this!**

She is pushed to the ground. The SOLDIER *walks off.* BRADSHAW *remains on her knees.* DEVONSHIRE *appears, with the* FOOTMAN. *She looks at her.*
DEVONSHIRE.   I was shagged. You were shagged. I am pregnant. You are pregnant. I do not know the father, and I warrant, no more do you. It is a shambles being a woman. I would chuck it all up if I met a doctor who could do the trick. *(She starts to go.)*
BRADSHAW.   Use me.
DEVONSHIRE.   How, dear? I have no need of a skivvy.
BRADSHAW.   I have a lifetime's cunning.
DEVONSHIRE.   You were not cunning enough to keep someone's cock out of your purse.
BRADSHAW.   Give me one month as your housekeeper, and I will save you my wages by cutting the rest.
DEVONSHIRE.   You could not pay them less than me. They'd scarper.
BRADSHAW.   People will always go beyond the point they say they stick at. I will bring you change on payday, watch.
DEVONSHIRE.   You are certainly persistent.
BRADSHAW.   I will manage servants as only one who's grovelled knows how to. A duchess really has no idea how to use a servant. Even her blows are full of charity. Trust me. *(Pause.* DEVONSHIRE *scrutinizes her.)*
DEVONSHIRE.   If you give birth I will not have it on the premises. I hate the sound, you see.
BRADSHAW.   If I'm lucky it'll die.
DEVONSHIRE.   And take you with it, darling.
BRADSHAW.   Chuck me on the dungheap if it do.
DEVONSHIRE.   You have what I most appreciate in servants, a complete lack of self esteem. Follow us, and when we reach home, kick someone out an attic. *(She turns to go.)* What's in the bag?
BRADSHAW.   Only a few bits.
DEVONSHIRE.   You're not fond of possessions?
BRADSHAW.   No.
DEVONSHIRE.   I like my servants very Christian, who see the world as futile tinsel. Otherwise they're nicking. Sam, take her bag. *(*DEVONSHIRE *walks off.)*
FOOTMAN.   You cut my wage like fuck, darling. I am a sodding Christmas tree, dangling with grandads and crippled kids.
BRADSHAW.   Make it up from your subordinates.
FOOTMAN.   Like fuck I —
BRADSHAW.   Sam, be realistic.

FOOTMAN. **I ain't Sam to you.**
BRADSHAW. Or find another situation. I am the bitch now, and you're only pussy. Find a mouse to torture. *(She goes out, watched by* SHADE *and the* FOOTMAN. BALL *enters, with a bottle.)*
BALL. Quick, pink bum, or I'll crack your arse... *(*FOOTMAN *takes up the bag and goes.)* Oh, this is a country for shit lickers now. There is more lace than dinner. **Whose dog are you!**
SHADE. Stuff it, Andy.
BALL. Stuff yerself, I'm pissed on misery.
SHADE. Nothin' new.
BALL. Nothin' new, nothin' new! Oh, you skinny little shivvering hound, lock yer teeth for Christ's sake, I crave a decent conversation, even the conversation has deteriorated since I came back —
SHADE. Oh, yeah —
BALL. **It has, you spunk, it has!** And half the soldiers are in spectacles, some manhood has vanished —
SHADE. Oh, yeah —
BALL. **Foreskin it has!**
SHADE *(turning to go)*. Go under the bridge and have a kip with all the other pissed ol' cavaliers, I got a job to do —
BALL. **They have withdrawn our certificates!**
SHADE. I know, mate.
BALL. **I am no longer a King's man, what of that!** No, it is a weird thing but I loved this fucking nation, and what is it —
SHADE. Good question —
BALL. **Come 'ere I said what is it!**
SHADE *(stops)*. What?
BALL. The nation, you tit hair, what is it? Is it hills? Is it rivers? Is it scenery? You answer me.
SHADE. Buggered if I —
BALL. You answer me! Because it can't be people, can it? It can't be **you**. Because I wouldn't raise a fart for **you**. They have gone off, they have, I mean just look at **you** —
SHADE. Yer pissed, mate —
BALL. I am pissed, but I can look at you, and really you are a shambles of an English man, I say that — no offence intended — but to my mind you are not a man at all, you are something — *(He waves his hand vaguely.)* altogether — *(*SHADE *goes to leave.)* **I lost some lovely comrades in the war you cunt!** *(*SHADE *stops again.)* The nation, you see, is going down. Got to save the King, see? **Cut the gangrene out.**

SHADE *(nodding at him).* Okay, mate . . .
BALL *(suddenly tossing his bottle at the spike.)* Oh, you bleeders, where's my race?

The bottle strikes the spike and dislodges the trunk. It has barely touched the ground before BRADSHAW *appears, issuing a fine scream. She scoops up the remains and runs off with them.* SHADE *makes a futile gesture of resistance.*

SHADE. Hey — Hey —
BALL. Hey he says! **Oh, you great English bastard.** Hey, he says! *(He jeers.)*

Scene Four

A banquet. Guests, music, a wedding cake.

DEVONSHIRE. I do not want a husband.
CHARLES. No, but baby wants a dad.
DEVONSHIRE. You are the dad.
CHARLES. Oh, you'd believe any old rumour! I must say I can imagine nothing nicer than you and Hambro locked together in the bed. It takes the edge off my misery to inflict him with a bitch like you . . .
DEVONSHIRE. I hate you, Charles.
CHARLES. No, it's only passion back to front . . .
NODD *(passing).* Cheer up, darlin', Charlie'll still slip yer one, won't yer, Charlie, if yer good. Chin up!
DEVONSHIRE. If there is one thing I hate above all others it is cheerful cockneys. Go into a corner and get pissed.
HAMPSHIRE. Gloria, you were never more beautiful.
DEVONSHIRE. Oh, don't be a silly old liar. *(She turns to CHARLES.)* Charlie, call it off.
CHARLES. Who says I ain't a mighty mover of destinies, flinging cold-bummed bankers down with Lady Roaring Hips? These old republicans will fuck shears for an earldom.
DEVONSHIRE. Call it off.
CHARLES. I could lie beneath the mattress just to hear old Hambro grieve. Will he shove sovereigns up your slit? Tell all, won't you, and call the infant Ajax, you must admire its tenacity, no prod or quinine's shaken it, nor baths in boiling cowshit, I believe.
DEVONSHIRE. I hate its guts.
CHARLES. No!
DEVONSHIRE. I tell you I do.
CHARLES. Wait till it's grinning at your tits.
DEVONSHIRE. I will pinch its little pink bum.
CHARLES *(drifting away).* Oh blimey, Gloria, what pleases you?
BRADSHAW. Don't be angry with me. You look beautiful.
DEVONSHIRE. I don't want Hambro touching me. Has he promised? Has he sworn?

BRADSHAW.   I have his assurance.
DEVONSHIRE.   Good.
BRADSHAW.   You are so perfect I could kiss you myself.
DEVONSHIRE.   Do, then. *(BRADSHAW kisses her.)* Do you like me very much?
BRADSHAW.   Yes.
DEVONSHIRE.   I sometimes think I am unloved.
BRADSHAW.   How could you?
DEVONSHIRE.   And my life stinks.
BRADSHAW.   Never.
DEVONSHIRE.   I have no bloody friend but you. It is my day and I never felt more like hanging myself.
BRADSHAW.   Wedding nerves. I wanted to hang myself.
DEVONSHIRE.   Really? Promise me!
BRADSHAW.   Oh, yes hanging wasn't half of it! And you are so lucky, he promises he will not pester you. This is a wedding you can really enjoy!
CLEGG *(passing).*   Her radiance doth dim the stars,
Come Hymen, banish Mars,
In splendid nuptial forget our wars,
Oh, lucky fate of Royal Whores!
DEVONSHIRE.   Sam, one of these days, I shall have you daggered in an alley . . . *(She turns, moves off.)*
CLEGG *(to* BRADSHAW*).*   Well, ain't you done well, miss, for an old red?
BRADSHAW.   I get by, Mr Clegg, thank you.
CLEGG.   Visit me again, and we'll piss over courts and all this lark, I got some lovely satires.
BRADSHAW.   No.
CLEGG.   Go on, I love your belly.
BRADSHAW.   Very well. I have to be consistent.
CLEGG.   Good. *(as he moves off.)* By the way, they took your Mr Scrope for calling God a liar. But Milton's safe. *(He advances towards* HAMBRO *who enters.)*
Bring gold, bring silver to her feet,
Dives of our day we humbly greet!
CHARLES *(greeting* HAMBRO *and his best man,* MCCONOCHIE*).*   Oh, Billy, ain't you smart and passionate! Let me kiss your hungry face! *(He embraces him.)* Be sweet to my daughter — **and don't sodomize heı you floppy catkin** — I call her my daughter, well, why not, **I'm giving her away, ain't I?** Yer earldom don't give access to all her crevices — *(He sees* MCCONOCHIE.*)* Oh, and you brought your best-man! Clegg, got some verses for my favourite Scot?

MCCONOCHIE *(bowing).* Good day, sir.
CHARLES. Sam, lines for the great specialist!
CLEGG. Willingly — only — off the top of my head, I didn't come prepared —
NODD. Ain't that what yer paid for?
CLEGG *(with aplomb).* Where should we be,
If from Dundee,
Had not appeared this prodigy?
(Cheers and applause.)
To banish drips from sickly cocks,
McConochie, we kiss thy socks!
(Boos and applause.)
Top of my head, I said, didn't I!
MCCONOCHIE. Sir, I am deeply honoured by yer verse . . .
CHARLES. McConochie knows the pattern of our underneaths like a general knows a map of the terrain, don't you, know our **ins and outs**? No court in Europe's got the like of him. **Thank the prodigy, Ted!**
HAMPSHIRE. I do thank him —
CHARLES. No, thank him properly, down on yer knees —
MCCONOCHIE. Noo, noo, there is noo need —
HAMPSHIRE *(kneeling).* I thank him, I thank him —
CHARLES. **What is this rumour they want McConochie in Hanover!**
MCCONOCHIE. Oh, it's no a temptation to me, I —
CHARLES. **I shall have you in chains first!** *(He turns away.)* Oh, Gloria hangs back, sweet virgin, hurry to your husband's side! It brings tears to your eyes, don't it, I do think there is no better union than beauty and success! *(He draws her by the hand.)* I've seen weddings where the couple was both beautiful, no, rubbish, this is the **raw old union of gain and expediency!**
HAMBRO. She moves with the grace of ten heifers . . .
CLEGG. They come like angels out the cloud,
Breathless meeting of the shy and proud,
In aristocracy unite the nation,
Flesh and gold's infatuation!

The couple offer a dry kiss. Applause.

PONTING. Speech! Speech!
CHARLES. Nodd! Fetch it! Fetch my present!
MCCONOCHIE. I call upon the Right Honourable, Sir William Hambro!
CHARLES. Oh, Gloria, do smile you bitch!
PONTING. Her uncle swears she is a virgin!

SOUTHWARK. Billy, I can hear a baby crying!
CHARLES. Yer speech! Yer speech!
SOUTHWARK. Wah, wah, wah! Wah, wah!
HAMBRO *(staggering).* I hate this — cock out — big balled — shagging lot —
PONTING. Christ, Hambro's pissed —
HAMBRO. I hope they all die of burst livers in some **snobby brawl!** Knocked down in some — vomit bucket — *(Cheers and abuse.)* Die like — bullocks rolling in the gore — eyes wild and — out of focus —
SOUTHWARK. Billy, watcha on about?
HAMBRO. **I'm speakin, aren't I?** Their old shag history going past their eyes — and dirty boots —
PONTING. Shuddup! *(Something is thrown.)*
HAMBRO. And dirty boots — going in — and in —
SOUTHWARK. Yer pissn' down yer leg, banker!
HAMBRO. **Dirty life and dirty death!** *(Roars of abuse.)* **I hate big arsed men who live like cattle!** *(Roars.)*
CHARLES. Billy's language comes out like the old red agitators, no wonder he don't drink too much . . .
HAMBRO. **I like my life —**
HAMPSHIRE. Yer lie to poke where yer mates have been —
HAMBRO. **No, you silly bugger, do you think I'm mocked?**
PONTING. I can hear a baby!
HAMBRO. **Oh, you great bullock, do you think I'm mocked by that? You aren't in your time and I am, see?** All that happens is as I want it, and everything suits me!
MCCONOCHIE. I think we cud move on now —
HAMBRO. **Every day I pick up the paper I shall say 'Good' See?** The smoothness of my time. My life without rage, see? *(He collapses into his chair as* NODD *brings in a large, wrapped object.)*
CLEGG. This gift to you from he who reigns,
Reminder of old times and gains,
The spirit of lost dreams retrieves,
The muse of History giggles in her sleeve!
DEVONSHIRE. This is something horrible.
CHARLES. Nobody says that Billy made it easy, he did not! While others passed him, spraying brilliance, Billy crawled, fly on the pane, silent progress of his sticky feet, the rockets fell back past him, spent, but did not shake him, the fly in history. Nobody laughs at flies.
DEVONSHIRE. What is this.

CHARLES. Open it.
DEVONSHIRE. I don't want to —
CHARLES. Open it!
HAMBRO *takes the string from* DEVONSHIRE, *and he pulls it. The wrapping falls from the figure of* SCROPE, *his lips cut off, around his neck a massive copy of 'Harmonia Britannia'.*
DEVONSHIRE. Is that supposed to be funny?
CHARLES. Funny? I did not say it was funny. I said it was a present. Does a present have to be funny? It is a **sad present.** I have invented the **sad present.** Thank me, Billy, for inviting an old colleague whose name was somehow left off the list of guests. *(He turns to* SCROPE.*)* If you can't come as a guest, you shall come as a present. He was caught saying God did not exist. **He does exist, he's over there!** *(He looks at* HAMBRO.*)* Billy, do welcome him, he is the most famous note-taker in history. There will be girls with books of shorthand on their knees and ignorant, oh, ignorant, of what a great forebear they had in him! **This was England's greatest secretary,** wrote down in his copperplate **off with my old dad's head.** Remember, Billy, you was there . . .?
DEVONSHIRE. Get him out.
CHARLES *(To* SCROPE*).* Speak, can you? Tell us what you know of the filthy act of History? *(He cups his hand to hear.* SCROPE *hesitates.)* Mmm? Can't hear yer, mm?
SCROPE. a — a — er — ee —
CHARLES. Mmm?
SCROPE. Arr — the —
CHARLES. Come again?
SCROPE. **Long liff the commonwealth ohh equals!**
CHARLES. Oh, no, that's old stuff, ain't it —
SCROPE. **Down wiff the sin ohh money and monarchy!**
CHARLES. Oh, dear, I never asked him to say this!
SCROPE. **Long liff the atheist re — hub — lic!**
CHARLES. Stop spoiling Billy's banquet with all this old stuff, really, it was a youthful abberation, wasn't it, **this old red muck!**
SCROPE *(in tears and frustration).* **The sin off kings — disease of riches —**
BRADSHAW. Shut up.
SCROPE *(seeing her).* **Aaagggghhheddawaay!**
BRADSHAW. Just shut up.
SCROPE *(recoiling from her).* **Aaaggghhhheddaway!**
BRADSHAW. What do you think you've got there, dignity? Really, I have

seen some idiots, crashing about the doorposts of time and history, shouting out their old abuse, but you, what have you discovered, your **manhood** or something? You absurd thing, you should be nailed to a board. **Shut up.** *(She looks around.)* Excuse me. No. I'm perfectly all right. Well, I am, aren't I? Look, I have clean drawers on, courtesy of madam, starched underthings. And lips. Not rose bud. Not what they were, of course, but lips. *(She curtsies, turns away.)*
CHARLES.   Kiss the bride, then, Billy —
BRADSHAW.   Lips . . .
CLEGG.   Of such unions as this,
Shall spring the race none can resist,
Throughout the globe,all under heaven,
Raise the cry, the Earl of Devon!
ALL *(toasting)*.   The Earl of Devon!
HAMBRO.   It's my thing in her belly. *(Pause. He looks around.)* It's my thing in her belly.

Pause. Then CHARLES *leads a cheer.* HAMBRO *smiles, suddenly one of the servants flings off his wig and is revealed as* BALL. *He rushes forward and stabs* HAMBRO *in the back.* HAMBRO *falls across the table.*

BALL.   **I save the King! I save the King! Cavaliers and Stuarts, Ho!** *(Uproar.* BALL *climbs on the table.)* **I stand in blood of rubbish! Church and King! Parliament is abolished, we have struck for England and the monarchy. Keep still there, play the anthem, send out messengers to every village, ring the bells!** *(Nobody moves.)* **Ring the bells, then!** *(There is no response.)* **Charles Stuart, be a King!** *(*CHARLES *doesn't move.)* **England calls you! Be a King!** *(Silence.)* Come on, then. *(Pause.)* Come on, I have liberated yer. *(Pause.)* Oh, come on, be a **fucking monarchist.** *(There is no response.* BALL *lets out a terrible wail.)*
CHARLES.   Drink my health and get off the table. *(*BALL *sways, closing his eyes, he drops the dagger. Men close round him and haul him off the table.)*
DEVONSHIRE.   Oh, God! Susan! I miscarry, oh!

A second uproar. BALL *is hauled out.* DEVONSHIRE *borne out as* CHARLES *sweeps from the room, followed by the assembly, who remove* HAMBRO's *body.*

DEVONSHIRE.   Susan! *(*BRADSHAW *does not move. She finds herself alone in the room but for* MCCONOCHIE. *He stares at her.)*
MCCONOCHIE.   A'm dooin' verry well here, as ye can see . . . *(Pause.)* Ye ken A noo relish the idea o' discovery . . . *(Pause.)* It's noo more than a —

(Suddenly BRADSHAW *flings herself into his arms, crushing him in an embrace.)* A'd be grateful therefore, if ye — *(She sobs.)* Wuld ye be so kind as — *(She kisses him.)* A have noo desire to be — *(Suddenly he dissolves into tears.)* Noo — noo — noo —
BRADSHAW. shh...
MCCONOCHIE. A canna — canna —
BRADSHAW. Shh...
MCCONOCHIE. A want a muther, A want a muther!
BRADSHAW, You mustn't, no —
MCCONOCHIE. A do! A do!
BRADSHAW. You must not weaken, you must not weaken — *(She weakens herself, kissing him.)*
MCCONOCHIE. **A hate this place ...**

CHARLES *enters, unaware of them.* BRADSHAW *puts her hand over* MCCONOCHIE's *mouth, pushes him off.* CHARLES *holds up* BRADSHAW's *head in his hands.*

CHARLES. Oh, Billy, we are standing in your blood ... *(He kneels by it.)* Drink, Dick, at the puddle of yer enemies... *(He holds the head to the blood. He begins to weep, then to laugh.)* This ain't remorse, only when I'm depressed it looks like it ... *(*BRADSHAW *makes a movement.* CHARLES *turns.)* **Who's that!**
BRADSHAW. Me ...
CHARLES. The cavalier, he thought he stabbed for me ... he loved something I'm only pretending ... *(He goes towards her.* BRADSHAW *winces at the sight of the head, recoils a moment.)* Don't be like Gloria ... if you listen to me I'll give you a bit of Surrey ... I am terribly cold, hold my fingers in your lap ... *(She takes his hand. They sit on the floor.)* Have you a child there? I have no children I dare acknowledge, the queen's womb's like a walnut, I felt it with my tip once, have you heard I got a melancholy character?
BRADSHAW. Yes ...
CHARLES. So I never know if I am talking sense or it's the membranes shifting, there must be some truth, mustn't there, or is it all biology? I don't think anybody cares whether monarchs live or die now —
BRADSHAW *(recovering).* Oh, don't say that —
CHARLES. No, no, don't be shallow, don't make soft replies, the cavalier, he knew after my dad there would be no English monarch would do anything but tickle crowds for bankers, I looked in that man's eyes and I was all humiliation, may I touch your belly? It's round as a football. I think a woman in late life and pregnant is a precious sight, look, the light is going, say no if

you want to, I am sick of forcing women ... *(She strokes his head.)* Pity me, will you? I make you very gently, I am no rocking billy, overlook my shallowness if I say that I love you, but I do now, you kind woman ...

CHARLES *falls asleep on her. With infinite caution,* BRADSHAW *extricates herself, covers the sleeping figure with a cloak. She is about to pick up the head when she is aware of* MCCONOCHIE *looking at her. He seems to shudder, then turns away in disgust. There is a pause of ultimate tension before* MCCONOCHIE *walks off.* BRADSHAW *takes up the head, covers it and is about to leave when the sound of jangling keys is heard, the* FOOTMAN, *now a janitor, appears.*

FOOTMAN. Lockin' up. *(Looking away.* BRADSHAW *attempts to pass.)* Oi. *(She stops.)* For six months I 'ave 'ad no work, you cow. *(She looks at him. Suddenly, he strikes her violently.* BRADSHAW *forces her hand to her mouth to prevent a cry. He forces her to the ground and beats her. She utters no sound. He finishes, jangling the key.)* Lockin' up. *(*BRADSHAW *staggers out.)*

Scene Five

The garden in Suffolk. CROPPER *is standing in an apron.* BRADSHAW *enters carrying a sleeping baby in her arms. She leads, by a rope, the broken figure of* BALL, *who himself is carrying the bag of remains. They halt.*

BRADSHAW. What have they done to my house?
CROPPER. Burned it. *(Pause. She looks at* BALL.*)* Who is that?
BRADSHAW. My husband. *(She shrugs.)* He wasn't always like that, but they put him on a rack. Well, they had to find out, didn't they, if he was a conspiracy? He was a conspiracy, but a conspiracy of one. In some ways I prefer him now. He was awfully — boisterous — before. I came here because — because there is nowhere to go in the end, but where you came from, is there?
CROPPER *(going to* BALL*).* Welcome. Would you care for a drink?
BRADSHAW. They had his tongue out, by special order of the King. It was very good of him, the magistrates were out to get him chopped. I mean, he killed a banker. All the bankers were ... frothing ... you can imagine ...
CROPPER. Forgive me if I —
BRADSHAW. Yes —
CROPPER. If I — rather hate you for a minute —
BRADSHAW. Yes —
CROPPER. To go away and then —
BRADSHAW. Come back —
CROPPER. As if —
BRADSHAW. Absolutely, yes — do get him a drink, having no tongue his mouth gets all — *(*CROPPER *goes out.* BRADSHAW *goes to fetch the bag off* BALL, *who makes a clumsy grab for her.)* Yes ... yes ... *(She laughs, he grunts.* CROPPER *reappears with a glass. She watches, uneasy.)* Oh, don't be frightened, it's me he loves. *(She gives him the water.* BRADSHAW *drops the bag down.)* I brought Bradshaw back. *(*CROPPER *turns in horror. Pause.)*
CROPPER. You —
BRADSHAW. In the bag. The dad. *(Pause.)* Well, look at it. *(*CROPPER *shakes her head.)* Oh, listen, I have been put to some little inconvenience retrieving that — *(She shakes it again.)* Look at it, then! *(Pause.* CROPPER *concedes, looks in the bag. Closes it again.)*

CROPPER. It is not him.
BRADSHAW. Who is it then?
CROPPER. It is not —
BRADSHAW. It's not? It is! Don't tell me I don't know my own —
CROPPER. It's bones!
BRADSHAW. Yes, of course it's bones, what did you expect? It's bones, obviously. Naturally, it's bones —
CROPPER. And he —
BRADSHAW. What's wrong with bones? Have you some allergy to bones?
CROPPER. **It is not that.** *(Pause.)* I learned Latin.
BRADSHAW. Latin. What's that?
CROPPER. I read his book. By night. Run my dirty finger through the words. Mice in the skirting. Husband groaning in his kip. The sentence coming to me like a birth in the pale morning. I am translating it. 'Harmonia Britannia'. I am printing it. *(Pause.)*
BRADSHAW. Oh, look, it's raining ...
CROPPER. Quickly, come to the house. *(Thunder.* BRADSHAW *doesn't move.)* Give me the child, quick ...!

BRADSHAW *does not move.* CROPPER *takes the baby from her, hurries away. After a few moments* BRADSHAW *goes to* BALL, *puts her arm round him. She pulls a scarf over his head, then they go, clasped together, towards the house.*